2/2013

PSYCHOLOGY RESEARCH PROGRESS

PSYCHOLOGICAL SKILLS IN SPORT

TRAINING AND APPLICATION

PSYCHOLOGY RESEARCH PROGRESS

Additional books in this series can be found on Nova's website
under the Series tab.

Additional E-books in this series can be found on Nova's website
under the E-book tab.

SPORTS AND ATHLETICS PREPARATION, PERFORMANCE, AND PSYCHOLOGY

Additional books in this series can be found on Nova's website
under the Series tab.

Additional E-books in this series can be found on Nova's website
under the E-book tab.

PSYCHOLOGY RESEARCH PROGRESS

PSYCHOLOGICAL SKILLS IN SPORT

TRAINING AND APPLICATION

BORIS BLUMENSTEIN

AND

IRIS ORBACH

Nova Science Publishers, Inc.

New York

NOTICE TO THE READER

The Publisher has taken reasonable care in the preparation of this book, but makes no expressed or implied warranty of any kind and assumes no responsibility for any errors or omissions. No liability is assumed for incidental or consequential damages in connection with or arising out of information contained in this book. The Publisher shall not be liable for any special, consequential, or exemplary damages resulting, in whole or in part, from the readers' use of, or reliance upon, this material. Any parts of this book based on government reports are so indicated and copyright is claimed for those parts to the extent applicable to compilations of such works.

Independent verification should be sought for any data, advice or recommendations contained in this book. In addition, no responsibility is assumed by the publisher for any injury and/or damage to persons or property arising from any methods, products, instructions, ideas or otherwise contained in this publication.

This publication is designed to provide accurate and authoritative information with regard to the subject matter covered herein. It is sold with the clear understanding that the Publisher is not engaged in rendering legal or any other professional services. If legal or any other expert assistance is required, the services of a competent person should be sought. FROM A DECLARATION OF PARTICIPANTS JOINTLY ADOPTED BY A COMMITTEE OF THE AMERICAN BAR ASSOCIATION AND A COMMITTEE OF PUBLISHERS.

Additional color graphics may be available in the e-book version of this book.

LIBRARY OF CONGRESS CATALOGING-IN-PUBLICATION DATA

Psychological skills in sport : training and application / Boris Blumenstein and Iris Orbach, editors.
   p. cm.
Includes index.
ISBN 978-1-62081-640-0 (soft cover)
1. Sports--Psychological aspects. I. Blumenstein, Boris. II. Orbach, Iris.
GV706.4.P6815 2012
796.01'9--dc23
                                  2012013584

Published by Nova Science Publishers, Inc. ✛ New York

This book is dedicated to our parents and our families.
Without their continual support, this book would not have been born.
We love them all very much.

BB and IO

CONTENTS

PREFACE

Maurice Greene, the famous American sprinter, holder of four Olympic medals and five World Championships, experienced the following during his first Olympic Games: "I was messed up, man, my nerves were all over the place. I tried to drink a glass of water, and my hand was shaking" (Layden, 2000, p. 46). This example illustrates the importance of mental preparation, no matter what the expertise level of the athlete.

In 1988, Robin Vealey emphasized in her article "Future directions in psychological skills training," the importance of mental factors as a significant part of an athlete's training. Continuing with this trend, over the past 30 years, the scientific basis for effective psychological interventions has been developed, and they have become an integral part of the athlete's preparation in many countries. Nowadays, sport psychology consultants in the Olympic Village are common and well liked. Currently, the challenge is to understand how to teach, apply, and transfer mental strategies during competitive stress. That is the major objective of our book. The idea of the book was already born in 2004, after the first author (BB) provided psychological services to the Israeli Olympic Delegation for the Athens Olympics. Throughout the years, BB checked and developed the significance and the uniqueness of the approach. After 2008, when the second author (IO) joined BB's department of behavioral sciences at the Wingate Institute, we continued to develop and use this skill-oriented method. This led to the formation of the three-dimensional approach, Learning-Modification-Application (LMA), suitable for different athletic skill levels and sport disciplines.

The present book is divided into three chapters. The purpose of Chapter 1, "The Sport Training Process: Psychological Perspectives," is to describe different elements of the athletic training program, as well as various preparations via the concept of periodization. Psychological preparation is discussed in terms of its role as an integral part of the sport training program. Chapter 2, "Psychological

Factors Associated with High Performance," describes mental aspects related to peak performance. The psychological skills required for the best athletic execution in various sports are discussed. Finally, in Chapter 3, "Developing Psychological Skills: A Three-dimensional approach," we present an innovative psychological skills training program that is based on our personal consulting experience. Using real examples, we demonstrate the internal structure of psychological skills training as used by athletes at all skill levels.

In closing, it is our hope that the present book will be a major resource for those who are interested in sport psychology training. Finally, we wish to thank the Nova Science Publishers and Ms. Dinah Olswang from the Zinman College at the Wingate Institute, who has been part of our professional team for the language editing of this book. Special thanks are due to the athletes and the coaches, especially to the Elite Sport Department of the Wingate Institute, without whom this book would not be a reality. Finally, special thanks to the fine editorial staff at Nova Science Publishers for their efficiency and thoroughness in overseeing the production process for this book.

REFERENCES

Layden, T. (2000, Oct. 2). The start of something big: Marion Jones's drive for five began brilliantly in the 100, then came news that her husband had failed a drug test. *Sports Illustrated,* 40-47.

Vealey, R. (1988). Future directions in psychological skills training. *Sport Psychologist, 2,* 318-336.

Chapter 1

THE SPORT TRAINING PROCESS: PSYCHOLOGICAL PERSPECTIVES

SUMMARY

The purpose of this chapter is to describe different elements of an athletic training program, as well as various preparations using the periodization concept. Psychological preparation is discussed in terms of its role as an integral part of the sport training program. Moreover, approaches for improving psychological preparation are analyzed. Based on scientific research and personal experience from five summer Olympic Games, the authors have presented recommendations for sport psychology consultants, coaches, and athletes.

INTRODUCTION

Competitive sport is oriented toward excellence and requires modern theories and methodologies of sport training, together with high motivation to train hard utilizing advanced scientific/medical support. In addition, physical talent and the athletes' endowments are basic and necessary aspects for a successful athletic carrier (Gould, Dieffenbach, & Moffett, 2002; Hardy & Parfitt, 1994). However, to achieve the best results in sport competitions under stressful conditions, a significant component in athletic preparation is derived from psychological factors.

Glen Mills, coach of the Jamaican sprinter, Usain Bolt, shared with business leaders the importance of psychological state on Usain's gold medal performances at the 2008 Beijing Olympic Games:

> "Over the years he (Usain Bolt) has developed mental skills. I taught him to visualize and always see himself wining regardless of who he competes against. If success is in your subconscious, it is a part of you. So when you see people, you see people you are going to beat. If you are nervous, you visualize failure. If you visualize winning, you have fun..." (Howard, September 14, 2011).

The scientific literature, as well as practical experience, indicate the major psychological factors associated with successful athletic performance:

- Mood states (e.g., Morgan, 1979; Raglin, 2001);
- Personal characteristic and cognitive strategies (e.g., Mahoney & Avener, 1977; Smith, Schutz, Smoll, & Ptacek, 1995).
- Psychological skills (e.g., Hardy, Jones, & Gould, 1996; Taylor, Gould, & Rolo, 2008).

Summarizing these studies, it is clear that psychological skills and cognitive and behavioral strategies have been linked with high-level athletic performance, including Olympic performance.

Moreover, personal factors and characteristics of athletes can also influence their preparation (Gould & Maynard, 2009). Sport psychology research and practice has provided the concrete psychological skills and strategies needed for athletic development and success; several researchers have investigated how elite athletes develop their psychological and sport talents (e.g., Cote, 1999; Durand-Bush & Samela, 2002; Gould, Greenleaf, Chung, & Guinan, 2002). They found that the development of elite athletes is a long-term process, both athletically and psychologically, including a strong coach-athlete relationship and parental support.

Moreover, other research has found that psychological preparation is a long-term procedure, linked with modern training processes concerning the talented individual athlete, a strong support system, and accordingly, preparedness through sport psychology consulting. This process is an integrative part of general athletic preparation in which an athlete develops as a person and as an athlete with specific skills, knowledge, and psychological characteristics (see Balague, 2000; Blumenstein, Lidor, & Tenenbaum, 2007; Weinberg & Williams, 2001).

To cope with hard, monotonous training and stressful competition conditions, athletes develop different physical, technical, tactical, and psychological skills. To develop psychological skills, different psychological strategies/interventions must be applied. When this is done, athletes ideally achieve a "condition that is related to optimal psychological state and peak performance either for competition or practice" (Gould, Flett, & Bean, 2009, p. 53).

Achievement in different sports requires a unique combination of psychological skills. For example, optimal performance in basketball requires flexibility in concentration, self-regulation, and good communication skills; best possible performance in shooting is related to narrow concentration, self-talk, and a high level of confidence; and top performance in swimming is linked with internal concentration and muscle relaxation. For example, the coach of Michael Phelps (the multiple Olympic gold medal winner in swimming), Bob Bowman, says that structured relaxation has been a part of Phelps' pre-race routine since he was 12 years old and is a key to his success. Bowman introduced Phelps to progressive relaxation, which among other practices, includes a recitation of cues (Crouse, 2009).

To mentally prepare the athlete for high-level competition, psychological skills training (PST) has been developed. Recently, practitioners agree that PST is linked with theory and methodology of sport training, as well as with other preparations: physical, technical, and tactical. The main tools of PST are psychological techniques/strategies. The positive effect of PST on athletic performance has been shown in research and practical contexts (e.g., Gould & Maynard, 2009; Vealey, 2007). It is recommended that PST be used in competition and training settings. However, psychological strategies are being applied more in competitions and less, or not systematically, in training regimes (Blumenstein & Orbach, 2012; Frey, Laguna, & Ravizza, 2003).

A major obstacle while working on psychological strategies/techniques is the difficulty in transferring these skills from the lab to the field. For a successful transfer, we recommend modifying the strategies accordingly to training periodization, sport specificity, and the athletes' psychological characteristics. These subjects will be discussed in the following chapters.

Sport training: A multi-faced process. A typical training structure for athlete is comprised of four different preparations: physical, technical, tactical, and psychological (Bompa, 1999; Bompa & Haff, 2009; Carrera & Bompa, 2007; Issurin, 2007). Each of these preparations is interrelated to the other preparations and is based on sport discipline objectives (Figure 1.1).

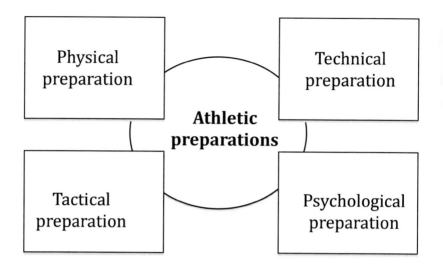

Figure 1.1. Athletic preparations.

The **physical preparation** is a main part of sport training. In the theory and methodology of sport training, physical preparation is composed of General Preparation (GP) and Specific Preparation (SP). The objective of GP is to improve fitness components, including the athletes' strength, endurance, flexibility, speed, and coordination. The GP is characterized by monotonous training, such as weight lifting practice with a high number of repetitions, and interval and distance running training (Blumenstein, et al., 2007; Bompa, 1999).

The objectives of SP are to achieve an increase in relative and absolute strength, an increase in muscle mass and specific strength, faster reaction time, and an improvement in coordination. In modern sports, the time invested in GP has decreased, while the time and volume invested in SP has increased (see Issurin, 2007). One of the reasons for this is the increase in the number of competitions per season, resulting in a longer competitive season.

Technical preparation is a necessary component of athletic preparation, and it has a significant place in the athlete's daily training, especially in specific preparation and competition. The aims of technical preparation are to lead the athlete to perform all technical tasks correctly, to teach rational and economical performance, to allow the athlete to perform specific techniques under normal/varying circumstances, and to improve related sports techniques. In an athlete's career, his/her techniques are developed from the stage of novice to the stage of professionalism (e.g., in figure skating, rhythmic gymnastics, pole vault, basketball, synchronized swimming). According to Schack and Bar-Eli (2007), technical preparation is developed through four steps: (1) In the first step, the athlete **learns** the basic structure of the technique; (2) In the second step, the focus is on the **automation** of motion sequence; (3) In the third step, the athlete practices the stabilization of the technique and its **variable application**; and (4) finally, in the fourth stage, **technical styles** are extended and developed.

In **tactical preparation**, the athlete focuses on improving strategy by studying possible tactics of opponents, expanding optimal tactics within the athlete's abilities, perfecting and varying strategies, focusing on team formation, and developing game plan/competition strategy. In both individual and team sports, athletes are required to establish a strategy (general plan), which takes into consideration their opponents and their specific movements (e.g., tactics). This helps them to successfully carry out the general plan. For example, Michael Phelps comments on his mental strategy that he always had a plan of action, a game plan. He knew exactly what he wanted to do: "*I executed the plan, nearly to perfection*" (Crouse, 2009). Another example is derived from track and field. Victor Saneyev, three-time Olympic gold champion in triple-jump, developed his tactics for the Olympic finals in Munich, 1972, putting all his efforts into the first attempt (Saneyev, 1975, p. 39). In addition, during the tactical preparation, athletes and sport teams must prepare for possible competitive situations. Therefore, the sport psychology consultant uses video simulations, external artificial distractions, and fatigued conditions as part of the psychological training (Henschen, Statler, & Lidor, 2007).

Finally, the objective of the **psychological preparation** is to teach the athlete task-specific psychological techniques/strategies, which lead to optimum coping with emotional and mental barriers in training and competition. In team sports, psychological preparation also includes team formation and cohesion. The last two decades have seen a significant increase in PST and the integration of psychological preparation with the training process (Balague, 2000; Blumenstein, et al., 2007; Blumenstein, Lidor, & Tenenbaum, 2005; Holliday, Burton, Sun, Hammermeister, Naylor, & Freigang, 2008).

In Figure 1.2, the role of psychological preparation is presented. Today, most of the psychological support is carried out as an independent preparation (a), without taking into consideration the other training factors. However, to achieve the best results, we recommend an interrelationship and awareness of the physical, technical, and tactical parameters (b).

In addition, most psychological training today is provided in the laboratory setting. Therefore, often the situation is that the athlete and the coach do not know how to use the psychological skills in training and competition. As a result, the effectiveness of the psychological work can be relatively low. Research, as well as our practical experience with elite and non-elite athletes, have shown that the interrelation with other athletic preparations requires that some of the psychological work take place outside the lab (e.g., in a stadium, on the field, in the swimming pool, at sea, in a gym: see Blumenstein & Orbach 2012). Therefore, we recommended that the sport psychology consultant learns sport specificity and attends the trainings and competitions, so that he or she will understand the sport from the inside. Remember, however, that the sport psychology consultants are not coaches; they are helpers and an important part of the team. As a result, the effectiveness of the psychological support can significantly increase (Blumenstein & Orbach, 2012).

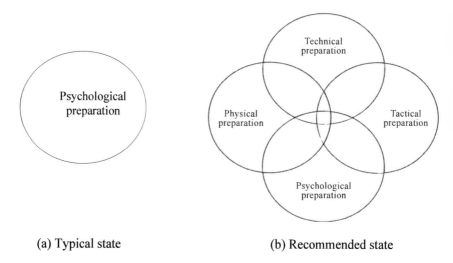

(a) Typical state   (b) Recommended state

Figure 1.2. Typical (a) and recommended (b) position of psychological preparation in the training process.

PERIODIZATION IN THE TRAINING PROCESS

Each of the four preparations is a part of the general athletic program that follows the basic training principles. Training programs require good planning in line with the main competitive events. To achieve top competitive form ("peaking") during a concrete time ("competition"), the athlete has to train and plan his/her efforts over a long period of time. Therefore, athletic preparation must be organized based on principles from the theory and methodology of sport training. One of the most important concepts in training and planning is the

periodization, which consists of three major periods: preparatory, competitive, and transition. This concept is not new to sport training and was founded in the former USSR during the 1950s. It was established in the mid 1970s (Matveyev, 1981; Ozolin, 1970), and was finally utilized in the mid 1980s in Western countries (see Bompa, 1984; Harre, 1982). Periodization is a key subject in sport training and in annual (seasonal) planning (short-term, medium-term, and long-term planning). One of the main principles of periodization is the cyclical manipulation of volume and intensity in training phases (see Figure 1.3). Each of the three phases of periodization (preparatory, competitive, transition) lasts through different time lengths, according to the sport's demands and the completion of one training cycle (Figure 1.3). For example, in a one-year training period (macrocycle), there can be one or more short training cycles (mesosycle – number of weeks; microcycle – one week or number of days).

Finally, the main goals of periodization are to strengthen the athlete's development over a period of many years and to enhance his or her achievement, minimizing such obstacles as injuries, overtraining, or other impediments to progress (Bompa,1999; Blumenstein & Weinstein, 2011).

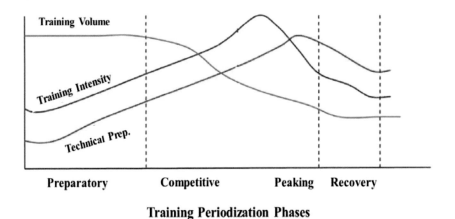

Training Periodization Phases

Figure 1.3. The three major phases in training periodization.

PSYCHOLOGICAL PREPARATION: GENERAL PERSPECTIVE

The psychological preparation is utilized in a unique way in each of the preparation phases. In the *Preparation Phase*, especially in the general preparation, the athlete has to perform a large number of exercise and repetitions with high volume and low and medium intensity. The length of the preparation phase is relatively short in soccer (1-1.5 months), longer in combat sports (three to four months), and even longer in track and field (four to five months). In *general preparation*, the athlete improves his or her general physical condition, including power, speed, flexibility, endurance, and some basic technical elements according to the type of sport. For example, the skier trains on general endurance and strength power, and the tennis/basketball player improves his or her general physical condition and techniques. An important point from the psychological perspective is the fact that athletes enter the general preparation phase after an active-rest period (transition) and start with regular daily training including special regimes and demands. Therefore, the sport psychology consultant has to focus during this period on two main goals: On one hand, the goal is to strengthen the athlete's sport motivation and goals for the upcoming season. On the other hand, the goal is to assist the athlete to recover after hard training. In addition, during this period, the sport psychology consultant can evaluate and improve the athlete's mental weaknesses, such as in concentration, self-regulation, and relaxation. In this period, we can learn additional basic psychological techniques/strategies. Specific goals and details on psychological techniques/strategies will be discussed in Chapter 3.

In *specific preparation*, the intensity of practice increases, and the number of repeated exercises substantially decreases. The athlete is exposed to a variety of actual environmental factors related to a competition situation. Therefore, the psychological techniques are performed under special stress distractions and are related to sport-specific demands. In addition, during this period, the athlete participates in some competitions; therefore the psychological work in the individual sport should focus more on parameters such as self-confidence, self-regulation, and concentration. In team sports, the psychological training centers on developing team cohesion, communication, leadership, group dynamics, and relationships among players. The sport psychology consultant takes part in athlete/team practice, introduces psychological techniques in training, identifies weaknesses in the athlete/team psychological preparation, and finally, optimizes the pre-competitive routine.

In this period, it is important to pay attention to the interaction among psychological, tactical, and technical preparations. It is especially important to pay attention to the *technical preparation*, in which mental and motor control takes a vital role. Therefore, the sport psychology consultant applies mental training, such as imagery training, which relates to the variability of the four steps of technical preparation. In order to prepare the athlete/team for real life situations, the techniques are practiced under different stress distractions

(Blumenstein & Weinstein, 2010; Blumenstein & Orbach, 2012). For more specific details regarding stress factors, see Chapter 3.

In the *Competitive Phase*, the athlete intensively participates in a variety of competitions. In individual sports, the athlete takes part in several competitions that prepare him or her for the main target competition, such as National, European and World championships, or the Olympic Games. In team sports, the athletes usually compete in national leagues, in which games are on a weekly basis for several months.

Therefore, the main training goals in this period are the following:

1) To improve the athlete's techniques and tactics, team communication and interaction, and team tactics;
2) To gain competitive experience;
3) To maintain general and specific physical conditions;
4) To cope with competition stress.

The ultimate goal of the sport psychology consultant in this period is to transfer most of the mental training from the laboratory to the field and to apply the psychological strategies in different training and competition situations. Moreover, the psychological strategies are modified to training and competition demands, such as the duration and specificity of the sport. Therefore, in this period, psychological skills are more related to the kind of sport, the actual environment factor of competition, and being an integral part of the pre-competitive routine (Blumenstein, et al., 2007; Blumenstein & Orbach, 2012).

CONCLUSION AND RECOMMENDATIONS

To summarize, psychological preparation is a significant part of athletic preparation. In reality, effective PST cannot stand alone and should be integrated with other athletic preparations. For the best integration, PST interventions should use the periodization principle developed in physical training. PST can be more effective when the sport psychology consultant is aware of the knowledge base in the theory and methodology of sport training and uses this knowledge in preparing athletes and teams for competition. This is especially reflected in the following two major points: (1) The interrelation of psychological preparation with other preparations (i.e., technical, tactical, and physical); and (2) The development of PST programs based on the periodization principle. To be effective, the sport psychology consultant should have the knowledge of the specific sport and experience in transferring PST from the lab to training and competitive settings.

REFERENCES

Balague, G. (2000). Periodization of psychological skills training. *Journal of Science and Medicine in Sport,* 3(3), 230-237.

Blumenstein, B., Lidor, R., & Tenenbaum, G. (2007) (Eds.). *Psychology of sport training.* Oxford, UK: Meyer & Meyer Sport.

Blumenstein, B., Lidor, R., & Tenenbaum, G. (2005). Periodization and planning of psychological preparation in elite combat sport programs: The case of judo. *International Journal of Sport and Exercise Psychology,* 3, 7-25.

Blumenstein, B., & Orbach, I. (2012). *Mental practice in sport: 20 case studies.* New York, NY: Nova Science Publishers.

Blumenstein, B., & Weinstein, Y. (2010). *Psychological skills training: Application to elite sport performance.* Grand Rapids, MI: Ultimate Athlete Concepts.

Blumenstein, B., & Weinstein, I. (2011). Biofeedback training: Enhancing athletic performance. *Biofeedback,* 39(3), 101-104.

Bompa, T. (1984). *Theory and methodology of training – the key to athletic performance.* Boca Raton, FL: Kendall/Hunt.

Bompa, T. (1999). *Periodization: Theory and methodology of training* (4th ed.). Champaign, IL: Human Kinetics.

Bompa, T., & Haff, G. (2009). *Periodization: Theory and methodology of training* (5th ed.). Champaign, IL: Human Kinetics.

Carrera, M., & Bompa, T. (2007). Theory and methodology of training: General perspectives. In B. Blumenstein, R. Lidor, & G. Tenenbaum (Eds.). *Psychology of sport training* (pp. 19-39). Oxford, UK: Meyer & Meyer Sport.

Cote, J. (1999). The influence of the family in the development of talent in sport. *The Sport Psychologist,* 13, 395-417.

Crouse, K. (2009, July 25). Avoiding the deep end when it comes to jitters. *The New York Times. http://www.nytimes.com/2009/07/26/sports/26swim.html? scp=1&sq=Phelps%20July%20%2026,%202009&st=cse.*

Durand-Bush, N., & Salmela, J. (2002). The development and maintenance of expert athletic performance: Perceptions of World and Olympic champions. *Journal of Applied Sport Psychology,* 14, 154-171.

Frey, M., Laguna, P., & Ravizza, K. (2003). Collegiate athletes' mental skill use and perceptions of success: An exploration of the practice and competition settings. *Journal of Applied Sport Psychology,* 15, 115-128.

Gould, D., Dieffenbach, K., & Moffett, A. (2002). Psychological characteristics and their development in Olympic champions. *Journal of Applied Sport Psychology,* 14, 177-209.

Gould, D., Flett, R., & Bean, E. (2009). Mental preparation for training and competition. In B.W. Brewer (Ed.). *Handbook of sport medicine and science: Sport psychology* (pp.53-63). Chichester, UK: Wiley-Blackwell.

Gould, D., Greenleaf, C., Chung, Y., & Guinan, D. (2002). A survey of U.S. Atlanta and Nagano Olympians: Factors influencing performance. *Research Quarterly for Exercise and Sport,* 73, 175-186.

Gould, D., & Maynard, I. (2009). Psychological preparation for the Olympic Games. *Journal of Sport Sciences,* 27(13), 1393-1408.

Hardy, L., Jones, G., & Gould, D. (1996*). Understanding psychological preparation for sport: Theory and practice for elite performers.* Chichester, UK: Wiley.

Hardy, L., & Parfitt, G. (1994). The development of a model for the provision of psychological support to a national squad. *Sport Psychologist,* 8, 126-142.

Harre, D. (Ed.) (1982). *Principles of sport training.* Berlin: Sportverlag.

Henschen, K., Statler, T., & Lidor, R. (2007). Psychological factors of tactical preparation. In B. Blumenstein, R. Lidor, & G. Tenenbaum (Eds.). *Psychology of sport training* (pp. 104-114). Oxford, UK: Meyer & Meyer Sport.

Holliday, B., Burton, D., Sun, G., Hammermeister, J., Naylor, S., & Freigang, D. (2008). Building the better mental training mousetrap: Is periodization a more systematic approach to promoting performance excellence? *Journal of Applied Sport Psychology,* 20, 199-219.

Howard, C. (2011, September 14). Three reasons why Usain Bolt would make a great businessman? In *Goal Setting for Success.* Retrieved October 10, 2011, from *http://thecornerstones.net/blog/3-reasons-why-usain-bolt-would-make-a-great-business-owner/.*

Issurin, V. (2007). A modern approach to high performance training: The block composition concept. In B. Blumenstein, R. Lidor, & G. Tenenbaum (Eds.), *Psychology of sport training* (pp. 216-234). Oxford, UK: Meyer & Meyer Sport.

Mahoney, M., & Avener, M. (1977). Psychology of the elite athlete: An exploratory study. *Cognitive Therapy and Research,* 1, 135-141.

Matveyev, L. (1981). *Fundamentals of sport training*. Moscow: Progress Publishers.

Morgan, W. (1979). Predication of performance in athletics. In P. Klavora & J. Daniel (Eds.). *Coach, athlete, and the sport psychologist* (pp. 173-186). Champaign, IL: Human Kinetics.

Ozolin, N. (1970). *The modern system of sport training*. Moscow: Physical Culture and Sport Publisher.

Raglin, J. (2001). Psychological factors in sport performance: The mental health model revisited. *Sport Medicine*, 31, 875-890.

Saneyev, V. (1975). *Steps to the pedestal*. Moscow, USSR: Physical Culture and Sport Publisher.

Schack, T., & Bar-Eli, M. (2007). Psychological factors of technical preparation. In B. Blumenstein, R. Lidor, & G. Tenenbaum (Eds.). *Psychology of sport training* (pp. 62-103). Oxford, UK: Meyer & Meyer Sport.

Smith, R., Schutz, R., Smoll, F., & Ptacek, J. (1995). Development and validation of a multidimensional measure of sport-specific psychological skills: The Athletic Coping Skills Inventory-26. *Journal of Sport and Exercise Psychology,* 17, 379-398.

Taylor, M., Gould, D., & Rolo, C. (2008). Performance strategies of U.S. Olympians in practice and competition. *High Ability Studies,* 19, 15-32.

Vealey, R.S. (2007). Mental skills training in sport. In G. Tenenbaum & R. Eklund (Eds.), *Handbook of sport psychology* (3rd ed.; pp. 287-309). New York, NY: Wiley & Sons.

Weinberg, R., & Williams, J. (2001). Integrating and implementing a psychological skills training. In J. Williams (Ed.), *Applied sport psychology: Personal growth to peak performance* (pp. 378-400). Mountain View, CA: Mayfield.

Chapter 2

PSYCHOLOGICAL FACTORS ASSOCIATED WITH HIGH PERFORMANCE

SUMMARY

This chapter describes psychological aspects associated with peak performance and the psychological skills required for the best athletic execution in various sports. In modern sports, athletes and coaches realize the importance of the psychological factors that play a role during peak performance at major competitions, or according and similarly to Rushall "…psychology is the key to sporting excellence…"(1989, p.165).

PEAK PERFORMANCE AND OPTIMAL STATE IN SPORT

Peak performance in sport is usually associated with a personal best result. During peak performances "… an athlete puts it all together - both physically and mentally" (Williams & Krane, 2001, p. 162). Based on personal observations from five Olympic Games and many years of experience, we have noticed that when athletes are at their "peak performance," many of them also report that they are at a period of high concentration and clear thinking. For example, Serena Williams, a U.S. tennis player (winner of four Wimbledon championships and two Olympic gold medals), portrays her peak performance as *"In Atlanta, when I won the gold, there were all those false starts. I don't even remember them. I just focused on what I had to do"* (Bailey, 2000). Bompa (1999) described peaking as the highlight of athletic shape, a special training state that is *"characterized by a high*

CNS adaptation, motor and biological harmony, high motivation, ability to cope with frustration, accepting the implicit risk of competing, and high self-confidence" (p. 95).

Sport scientists and coaches are always searching for different tools to enhance performance. In the 1950-60s, coaches believed that only good technical preparation was the key to peak performance. Later, in the 1970s, a new trend appeared in the athlete's preparation that focused on increasing specific physical preparation as the basis of peak performance. Today, many strong athletes are similarly prepared physically, technically, and tactically. However, only those who are the strongest mentally on that given day and time will win the event. Therefore, sport practitioners began to use knowledge from applied sport psychology critically and systematically.

Much research has attempted to determine the factors associated with peak performance by asking top athletes about their feeling and thoughts before and during peak performing (e.g., Cohn, 1991; Garfield & Benett, 1984; Loehr, 1984; Privette & Bundrick, 1997; Ravizza, 1977, 2001). This optimal mental state was also referred to as flow state (e.g., Csikszentmihalyi, 1990; Jackson, 2000), or individualized zone of optimal functioning (e.g., Hanin, 2000). It was agreed that athletes needed to attain this optimal state to make peak performance more possible. Moreover, sport psychologists established the general psychological characteristics that are typical to this "ideal body/mind state." A classic example for the ideal mental state is given by Williams and Krane (2001), as follows:

- High concentration (appropriately focused)
- Positive preoccupation with the sport event (imagery and thoughts)
- Self-regulation of arousal (energized yet relaxed without stressful distractions)
- High level of self-confidence
- In control, yet relaxed
- Determination and commitment to high performance.

Optimal mental state leads to better performance; however this state does not happen by itself. It follows a long and involved process during which athletes acquire the necessary skills that enable them to cope with competitive stress distractions and to achieve peak athletic performance (Gould & Maynard, 2009; Williams & Krane, 2001). Often, due to the high pressure, they cannot hear the coach's remarks from the outside or tune in reactions; their attention is fully devoted to the performance, and most of the athletes emphasize the vital role of psychological factors in their competitions. For example, Ben Ainslie from

Britain, four times Olympic gold sailing medalist said in an interview how he deals with the pressure of Olympic Games:

> "I can't imagine it gets much bigger than that in sport. It's a huge amount of pressure, but that's the same in every Olympics. The pressure from within to perform and reach your goals is huge and you have to deal with that. The external pressure will be bigger than ever. You have to be very ruthless about making sure you keep your mind on the job and the results, and try and ignore everything else" (Rossingh, 2011).

Achieving an optimal state in main competitions is an important component of peak performance and is beneficial for successful athletes. At the highest level, creating the optimal state or "being in the zone" is a crucial factor that separates winners from losers.

In this state, the body functions automatically, with little conscious attention and effort. Elite athletes have identified their own ideal mental states and have learned to create and maintain these states voluntarily with psychological skills and strategies. At the same time, coaches and athletes practice systematically on body improvement and may overlook psychological/mind factors. Accordingly, Williams and Krane (2001) report that peak performance is "...a product of the body and mind, and it can be trained. Just as improving physical skills, strategies, and conditioning increases the likelihood of peak performance, learning to control psychological readiness and the ideal mental climate for peak performance also enhances performance" (p. 175-176). This ideal performance state is linked with psychological skills that allow athletes at all levels of sport experience to cope with competitive stress distractions and to achieve peak athletic performance (Gould & Maynard, 2009; Williams & Krane, 2001). Gould, Flett, and Bean (2009) describe psychological skills/strategies that assist athletes "... to arrive at an ideal performance state or condition that is related to optimal psychological states and peak performance either for competition or practice" (p.53).

There are a number of psychological skills commonly used by elite athletes in their quests to achieve peak performance. These include imagery, goal setting, self-confidence, positive thinking, self-awareness, attentional focus, arousal control, and decision-making (Vealey, 2007; Williams & Krane, 2001). Additional psychological skills in various sports types will be discussed below.

PSYCHOLOGICAL SKILLS FOR PEAK PERFORMANCE IN VARIOUS SPORTS

An ideal performance state can be accomplished with the necessary psychological skills, which permit athletes in all levels of sport experience to cope with competitive stress distractions and to achieve peak athletic performance (Gould & Maynard, 2009; Williams & Krane, 2001) (see Figure 2.1).

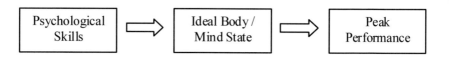

Figure 2.1. Schematic description of achieving peak performance.

During the past three decades, sport psychology researchers and applied psychologists have been focused on psychological skills and strategies that are essential for enhancing athlete performance (Gould, 2002; Gould & Damarjian, 1998; Gould & Maynard, 2009; Henschen, 2005; Orlick & Partington, 1988; Vealey, 1988, 2007). Top athletes were characterized by, among others, imagery skills (Orlick & Partington, 1988), ability to focus and to block distracters (Gould, Dieffenbach & Moffett, 2002), the ability to cope with and control anxiety (Gould et al., 2002), high confidence (Gould et al., 2002), and high personal drive, ego and motivation (Mallett & Hanrahan, 2004). One of the ten most successful U.S. Olympic champions who participated in confidential interviews with Gould, Deiffenbach, and Moffett (2010) said, "*... I think I worked really hard. There were a lot of athletes that might have been more talented than I was, but I think I was more determined. I wanted to reach my goals, and I wasn't going to let anything stand in my way.*" Vealey (1988, 2007) described a model of mental skills for athletes and coaches that includes foundation, performance, personal development, and team skills. Gould and Damarjian (1998) focused on learning skills and techniques that enhance elite athletic performance, among them, goal setting, stress management, and confidence enhancement. In addition, there is a particular need to develop codes of ethics, leadership, and goal-setting skills in young athletes. A series of studies performed by Gould and his colleagues examined psychological skills of elite (Olympic champions) sport performance (Gould, Dieffenbach, & Moffett, 2002; Gould & Maynard, 2009). These studies revealed that the best elite athletes were characterized by a high level of self-confidence, as well as the ability to cope with and control their anxiety and to focus and block out distractions. Williams and Krane (2001) investigated several specific mental skills that are associated with peak performance. Among these were skills to cope with distractions, concentration, high levels of self-confidence, self-regulation of arousal, and goal setting. Taking these studies together, sport psychologists and scientists have often discussed the following mental skills for the enhancement of athlete performance:

- ❖ Relaxation and arousal regulation (e.g., Statler & Henschen, 2009; Williams & Harris, 2001)
- ❖ Concentration (e.g., Moran, 2003; Vernacchia, 2003)
- ❖ Goal setting (e.g., Gould, 2001)
- ❖ Imagery (e.g., Suinn, 1993; Vealey, 1988; Vealey & Greenleaf, 2001, 2006)
- ❖ Self-confidence (e.g., Gould et al., 2002)
- ❖ Pre-performance mental routines (i.e., Cohn, 1990; Lidor & Singer, 2003; Statler & Henschen, 2009).

The effectiveness of these psychological skills for the enhancement of athletic performance has also been reported in studies by elite practitioners for different sports (e.g., Gould & Maynard, 2009; Vealey, 2007; Williams & Krane, 2001) (see Tables 2.1 a, b, c). These tables are based on our personal experience with the following three sport categories: individual, team, and combat. Psychological skills associated with successful performance in team sports (i.e., soccer, basketball and ice hockey) are discussed below (Table 2.1 a).

Table 2.1(a). Psychological skills associated with peak performance in team sport

Sport discipline	Psychological skills/strategies	Source
Soccer	Concentration Self-regulation Self-talk Positive thinking	Dosil, 2006a Moran, 2003 Lidor et al., 2007
Basketball	Imagery Concentration Self-talk Team cohesion Motivation Self-regulation	Burke, 2006, Burke & Brown, 2003 Henschen & Cook, 2003 Lidor et al.,2007
Ice Hockey	Focus flexibility and stability Emotional control Confidence and consistency Mental toughness Total commitment	Halliwell, 2009

Soccer is the most popular game in the world, where two teams of eleven players play against each other in an attempt to score by driving the ball into the opposing goal. The team that scores the most goals in the match wins. Therefore, field players are required to play in a coordinated defensive and offensive structure (Gray & Drewitt, 1999). To do this, players are expected to master individual defensive (e.g., positioning) and offensive (e.g., dribbling, kicking, and passing) skills, as well as defensive and offensive team skills. The psychological skills important in the game of soccer include the following: concentration, self-regulation, self-talk, and positive thinking (see Dosil, 2006a; Lidor et al., 2007).

Basketball is a game in which five players play against five opposing players under rapidly changing situations (Wooden, 1980). Basketball players spend a great deal of training time in improving physical abilities such as agility, speed, explosive power, and strength. During the game, players perform a variety of open offensive skills, such as dribbling, passing, and shooting. Moreover, cognitive processes such as anticipation and decision-making are applied in defensive maneuvers (Lidor et al., 2007). Therefore, concentration (Burke, 2006; Burke & Brown, 2003), self-talk (Henschen & Cook, 2003), and team cohesion, self-regulation, and motivation (Lidor et al., 2007) are required to maximize success in this sport.

Ice Hockey is a game played between two teams with six players on the ice at one time. Players use wooden or composite sticks to shoot a hard rubber puck into their opponents' net. Among the important psychological skills related to success in this game are: focus, "staying in the moment," controlling emotions and physical fatigue, confidence and consistency, and total commitment (Halliwell, 2009).

Psychological skills associated with success in individual sports such as track and field, swimming, artistic gymnastics, rhythmic gymnastics, golf, tennis, canoeing/kayaking, and combat sport (judo, taekwondo, fencing and wrestling) are discussed below (see Table 2.1b).

Track and field. According to Vernacchia and Statler (2005) and Statler and Henschen (2009), the following skills are of special importance to track and field athletes: composure, concentration, and confidence skills. However, we understand that the sprints, jumps, throws, and long-distance runs in track and field are not the same type of events. Each of these disciplines has unique psychological characteristics and specific demands. For example, in the 100m and 200m sprints, the reaction time constitutes a crucial factor; therefore, the psychological skills emphasized should be concentration and confidence to improve the swiftness of the start and to maximize performance during the sprint (Dosil, 2006b).

Table 2.1(b). Psychological skills associated with peak performance in individual sport

Sport discipline	Psychological skills/strategies	Source
Track and Field (general)	Composure Concentration Confidence	Vernacchia & Statler, 2005
Track and Field (specific): Sprint, long distance running, jumping, throwing, race walking	Concentration Confidence Self-regulation Visualization Thought control Comfortable pace Motivation	Dosil, 2006b Statler & Henschen, 2009
Swimming	Self-regulation of arousal Confidence Thought and feeling control Coach-athlete relationship Goal setting Visualization Relaxation Concentration	Hanton & Jones, 1999 Kerr, 2001 Philippe & Seiler, 2006 Sheard & Golby, 2006
Artistic Gymnastics	Focus Concentration via imagery Confidence building Anxiety control Mental relaxation	Cogan, 2006
Rhythmic Gymnastics	Goal setting Self-talk Self-confidence Attention-focusing via Imagery Mental relaxation Self-awareness	Lidor et al., 2007
Golf	Emotional control Imagery Self-talk Relaxation Attention control Performance-approach goal	Bois, Sarrazin, Southon & Boiche, 2009 Thomas, 2001
Tennis	Mental toughness Commitment Motivation Self-belief Confidence Attention control	Weinberg, 1988 Young & Pearce, 2009

Table 2.1(b). (Continued)

Sport discipline	Psychological skills/strategies	Source
Canoeing/Kayaking	Mental control Mental toughness Mental self-regulation Relaxation Focusing	Blumenstein & Bar-Eli, 2001 Blumenstein & Lidor, 2004 Lidor et al., 2007
Wind Surfing	Muscle relaxation Concentration Imagery Self-talk Self-confidence	Blumenstein & Orbach, 2012

Jumping and throwing events are typified by long breaks between attempts, and thus self-regulation skills, visualization, and thought control should be strengthened. Long-distance events (marathon and race walking) are characterized by long durations of physical effort, and athletes in these events may be confronted with several psychological barriers (e.g., 35 km for marathon, the" second" wind, etc.). The psychological traits include concentrating on a "comfortable" running pace, confidence, and composure skills, which should receive special attention during the preparation of these athletes.

In *Swimming*, athletes compete in four styles (i.e., freestyle, breaststroke, backstroke, and butterfly) in numerous distances ranging between 50m-1500m, depending on the style. Therefore, among important psychological skills and strategies for successful performance in swimming are focusing (Hanton & Jones, 1999), self-regulation of arousal, confidence (Kerr, 2001); thought and feeling control, coach-athlete relationship (Philippe & Seiler, 2006); and goal-setting, visualization, relaxation, and concentration (Sheard & Golby, 2006).

Artistic gymnastics is characterized by a high degree of mental power compared to other sports, in which there is highly-developed strength, grace, endurance, and persistence (Cogan, 2006). Female gymnastics competitions consist of four events: vault, uneven parallel bars (bars), balance beam (beam), and floor exercise (floor). Men's gymnastics includes six events: floor, parallel bars, high bar, pommel horse, still rings, and vault. Among the main psychological skills required for artistic gymnastics are focus (through imagery), confidence, anxiety control, and mental relaxation (Cogan, 2006).

Rhythmic gymnastics is a sport that combines elements of dance, ballet, and gymnastics, as well as requiring a high level of equipment manipulation. In individual female rhythmic gymnastics, the gymnasts perform a 90-sec routine, accompanied by selected music, in which one of five accessories is manipulated:

ball, club, hoop, ribbon, and rope. This event requires a demonstration of strength, balance, coordination, and flexibility, as well as a high level of accuracy (Lidor et al., 2007). In the team performance, five gymnasts perform for 2.5 min and exhibit their competitive performance accompanied by music. Rhythmic gymnastics requires the psychological skills of goal setting, self-talk, self-confidence, attention-focusing, mental relaxation, and self-awareness (Lidor et al., 2007).

Golf is a sport in which players spend a very short time actually hitting the ball, whereas moving across the course and waiting time represent the majority of the duration of a game. The successful golfer must develop emotional management skills (i.e., emotional control), imagery, self-talk, relaxation, attention control, and performance-approach goals (Bois et al., 2009; Thomas, 2001).

Tennis is a sport played between two players (singles) or between two teams of two players each (doubles). Athletes (male/female) play with a tennis racket that is strung to strike a hollow rubber ball covered with felt over a net into the opponents' court. There are eight basic shots an elite tennis player has to master: serve, forehand, backhand, volley, half-volley, overhand, drop shot, and lob. Researches have shown that the important psychological skills and strategies for successful performance in tennis are coping with anxiety, concentration, mental imagery, high motivation, self-confidence, goal-setting, commitment, and self-belief (Weinberg, 1988; Young & Pearce, 2009).

Canoeing/Kayaking is characterized by high endurance and speed, an explosive start, and the maintenance of high speed and tempo throughout the entire distance of the race (Blumenstein & Lidor, 2004; Lidor et al, 2007). Studies have shown that mental control, relaxation, mental toughness, focusing, and mental self-regulation are essential psychological skills required for peak performance in kayaking (Blumenstein & Bar-Eli, 2001; Lidor et al., 2007).

Windsurfing competitive performance involves high endurance and speed and is regulated by the opponents and meteorological conditions throughout the entire race. Often waiting for suitable weather, speed of decision-making and cognitive processes in different situations during a race impact athlete performance. Therefore, during the training process, windsurfers focus mainly on improving race course management and tactics, perfecting equipment handling and sailing technique, and developing a high level of physical fitness. Among the psychological skills and strategies important for successful performance in windsurfing are the following: muscle relaxation, concentration, imagery, self-talk, and self-confidence (Blumenstein & Orbach, 2012).

Combat sports (judo, wrestling, taekwondo, and fencing). Combat sport events share several specific characteristics and requirements of psychological skills. While in a high state of tension when striving to achieve the designated goals, the competing athletes must simultaneously attack and defend and at the same time conceal their intentions from the opponents. It is a challenge to make decisions under time pressure while facing aggressive opponents and to devise alternative tactical movements by using skills such as attention flexibility (Blumenstein, Bar-Eli, & Collins, 2002; Blumenstein, Lidor, & Tenenbaum, 2005). One of the characteristics common to Olympic combat situations shared by judo, taekwondo, wrestling, fencing, and boxing are the instantaneous changes occurring within brief time\ spans (e.g., 100 - 200 msec). Accordingly, emotional and mental states may be subjected to extreme and rapid fluctuations during combat fights.

While each of these sports has unique characteristics and its own history, all require several psychological skills such as psychological readiness, confidence, self-motivation for creativity, and self-regulation to maintain an optimal level of concentration and anticipation (Anshel & Payne, 2006) (see Table 2.1c).

Judo requires quick responses, with high levels of attention, self-control, consistency, and willpower during the five-min match (Blumenstein et al., 2005; Pedro & Durbin, 2001). Among the psychological traits that are important for judo are confidence, anticipation, concentration, and self-control, as well as the skill of self-talking (Anshel & Payne, 2006; Blumenstein et al., 2005).

Table 2.1(c) Psychological skills associated with peak performance in combat sport

Sport discipline	Psychological skills/strategies	Source
Judo, Taekwondo	Self-regulation Concentration Anticipation Self-talking	Anshel & Payne, 2006 Blumenstein et al., 2005
Wrestling	Narrow focus of attention Positive self-talk Self-confidence	Gould, Eklund & Jackson, 1993
Fencing	Attention Self-control Consistency Will power Decision–making	Blumenstein et al., 2005 Blumenstein & Orbach, 2012

Wrestling is the oldest combat sport in which two fighters attempt to gain and maintain a superior position. Competition in wrestling is provided in two disciplines: Greco-Roman and Freestyle wrestling. The best wrestlers are characterized by excellent physical condition and endurance and high technical and tactical preparations. Gould, Eklund and Jackson (1993), in their interview with twenty U.S. Olympic Greco-Roman and Freestyle wrestlers, found that medal-winning wrestlers were better able to narrow their focus of attention, engage in more positive self-talk, and use extensive mental practice than non-medal-winning wrestlers.

Taekwondo is primarily a self-defense sport, loosely translated as "the way of the hand and the foot" (Chung & Lee, 1994). It is a sport of both body and mind during competition and consists of three rounds, with two min when fighters fight each other and a one-min interval between rounds. Park and Seabourne (1997) suggested that one of the key demands in taekwondo is "*to achieve a state of mind in which the performer is acutely aware of the endlessly changing competition environment and can effortlessly react to such changes* "(p. 14). Among the psychological skills that are important for taekwondo are self-control, concentration, self-confidence, anticipation, and competitiveness (Anshel & Payne, 2006; Blumenstein et al., 2005).

Fencing. Competition in elite fencing requires quick responses as well as high levels of attention, self-control, consistency, and willpower (Blumenstein et al., 2005; Blumenstein & Orbach, 2012). Combat situations may often change within extremely short periods of time (e.g., 100 to 200 msec); accordingly, emotional and mental states are subject to extreme fluctuation during combat matches. It is difficult for the competing athlete to simultaneously attack and defend while concealing his/her intentions from the opponent and while in an extreme state of tension. It is not easy to make decisions under time pressure while facing aggressive opponents and to decide on alternative tactical movements (i.e., attention flexibility) – all while striving to achieve the designated goals (Blumenstein et al., 2002; Blumenstein et al., 2005). In order for psychological preparation for combat sports in general, and for fencing specifically, to be effective, it must target specific physical, technical, and tactical preparations.

To summarize this section, the following common psychological skills are typically used in different sports to achieve peak performance:

- ❖ Self-regulation of arousal
- ❖ Concentration
- ❖ Confidence
- ❖ Goal setting Relaxation

❖ Self-talk
❖ Imagery.

These commonalities in psychological skills are derived from the results of numerous studies of peak performance and from practitioners' reports. However, it should be emphasized that each sport has unique demands for psychological skills that may guarantee peak performance in this sport.

PSYCHOLOGICAL SKILLS AND MENTAL TRAINING TECHNIQUES

Traditional mental training techniques/strategies that have been widely used for psychological skill development include relaxation/arousal regulation, biofeedback training, imagery, goal setting, concentration, self-talk, and a pre-performance mental routine (Cotterill, 2010; Henschen, 2005; Lidor, 2007; Vealey, 2007). Unfortunately, most elite athletes do not make use of these techniques during their training (Frey, Laguna, & Ravizza, 2003). However, numerous research studies and evidence in practical experience have shown the effectiveness of mental training techniques on psychological skills development (Vealey, 2007).

Relaxation is a popular technique in sport and may be useful in helping athletes regulate their energy use in order to allow for peak performance (Vealey, 2007). Moreover, it has been reported that proper application of relaxation techniques may facilitate recovery from exercise (Vealey, 2007). This is particularly important in instances where athletes have only a short pause between fights or starts or when they are fatigued.

The ability to regulate physical energy or arousal levels is widely regarded as an important mental skill in sports (Gould & Udry, 1994). Not surprisingly, relaxation skills must be practiced on a systematic basis like any other traditional athletic training process.

The most popular and well-known relaxation techniques are "muscle-to–mind" techniques, such as breathing exercises and progressive muscular relaxation, introduced by Jacobson (1930), and other "mind-to-muscle" techniques such as autogenic training (Schultz, 1932), meditation, yoga, and hypnosis. These techniques have been widely described in numerous handbooks and instruction manuals (e.g., Henschen, 2005; Williams & Harris, 2001) and are extensively used in sport psychology practice.

Relaxation techniques are commonly used for recovery at the end of a practice day in rhythmic gymnastics, judo, fencing, soccer, and basketball; between fights in combat sports; and, as part of warm-up in track and field, swimming, tennis, and shooting. Moreover, relaxation is applied as a method to accelerate practice the day before competition. For example, we observed that biofeedback training and relaxation significantly enhanced athletic performance in a 100-m run (Blumenstein, Bar-Eli & Tenenbaum, 1995).

Biofeedback (BFB) – a technological advance in the treatment of stress-related disorders in which sophisticated electrodes and sensors are used to measure the athletes' mind/body activity. Scientific research and practice shows that BFB can be a powerful tool for initiating physiological change, such as increasing individual awareness and/or control over the body and reducing habitual physiological tension (Blumenstein, Bar-Eli, & Collins, 2002; Blumenstein & Weinstein, 2011; Zaichkowsky, 2009). BFB consists of training the athlete to change various physiological indices (e.g., muscle tension, heart rate, brain activity) and to regulate physiological states with instrumentation. According to the "psychophysiological principle" presented by Green, Green, and Walters (1970), every physiological change is accompanied by a parallel change in one's mental-emotional state, and conversely every mental-emotional change – conscious or unconscious – is accompanied by a physiological change. It is on this principle that biofeedback training is based. During BFB training, an athlete practices using software screens to self-regulate his/her physiological indices (e.g., heart rate, muscle tension or skin conductance) that tend to interfere with performance. The first researcher who proposed the use of BFB in sports was Leonard Zaichkowsky (1975). Today, BFB training is a very popular tool in applied sport psychology and is an efficient way to teach self-regulation, concentration, and relaxation in sports. Usually, to enhance athletic performance, BFB is combined with various psychological interventions (e.g., relaxation, imagery) and is presented as a part of a comprehensive mental preparation package (e.g., Wingate five-step approach; by Blumenstein, Bar-Eli & Tenenbaum, 1997).

Imagery is a popular mental training technique used by athletes (Morris, Spittle, & Watt, 2005). The benefits of this technique when used prior to competition were reported as improving performance (Vealey & Greenleaf, 2006), facilitating competition preparation (Morris et al., 2005), and enhancing physical, perceptual, and psychological skills (Vealey & Greenleaf, 2006). Imagery has been incorporated into many different Psychological Skills Training (PST) and models, such as visual-motor behavior rehearsal (VMBR; Suinn, 1984), the five-step strategy (Singer, 1988), and the Wingate five-step approach

(Blumenstein et al., 2002). Although the use of imagery may facilitate athletic performance in practice, similar to physical training, acquiring the psychological skill of imagery requires systematic practice. During our extensive experience, imagery was combined with relaxation and biofeedback training in a laboratory settings as well as part of the athletes' pre-competitive routines (Blumenstein & Orbach, 2012; Blumenstein & Weinstein, 2010).

Concentration refers to the ability of the athlete to focus and devote full attention to a specific task and not be distracted or affected by irrelevant exterior and inner stimuli (Moran, 1996). Concentration skill is often the key factor in athletic competition performance. According to Nideffer (1989), there are several concentration styles that all athletes should possess. These include broad external, narrow internal, narrow external, broad internal, and shifting styles. The concentration style that is applied is individually determined by the different sport and sport situation, the individual's ability to effectively concentrate, the physiological arousal state, etc. In order to develop concentration skills in applied sport psychology, we recommend the use of several techniques, such as:

- Goal setting ("performance goals") – focuses the mind on realistic task-relevant thoughts
- Pre-competitive (pre-performance) routines – the athlete is trained to concentrate only on what can be controlled
- Imagery – helps athlete to rehearse his/her goals and upcoming performance
- Self-talk ("triggers") – trains the athlete to re-focus quickly on task-relevant cues
- Arousal control – focus on body awareness
- Biofeedback training – helps the athlete to concentrate on his/her behavior based on instantaneous audio-visual physiological responses.

We have used these techniques widely in the laboratory and in field situations in different sports events, including rhythmic gymnastics, combat sports, basketball, soccer, shooting, tennis, swimming, and track and field.

Self-talk is another technique, in which athletes individually evaluate a given situation by a verbal dialogue providing self-instructions or reinforcement. Negative self-talk often leads to the anxiety or depression commonly associated with training and competition (Henschen, 2005). However, positive self-talk may be effective in enhancing different types of sport performance (Hatzigeorgiadis, Theodorakis, & Zourbanos, 2004).

We have made it clear to the athletes that our minds control our bodies and the manner in which we think and talk to ourselves in our minds dictates the directions that our bodies will take.

Therefore, we recommend that athletes remain in the present, use positive cues or trigger-words, and focus on their short-term and long-term goals. In doing so, their bodies will follow their thoughts.

Pre-performance routines bring together the applications of all the mental skills and strategies into a sport routine that enhances athletic performance. A mental routine is unique to each athlete and is made up of a combination of a number of mental skills (Henschen, 2005; Lidor, 2007).

Various aspects of pre-performance routines have been reported by sports scientists and applied sport psychologists (e.g., Cotterill, 2010; Lidor, 2007; Lidor & Singer, 2003; Schack, Whitmarsh, Pike & Redden, 2005; Singer, Hausenblas, & Jannelle, 2001).

The routine becomes an integral element of the athlete's repertoire in preparation for various competitions. Among the effects of a well-developed pre-performance routine are improving concentration, preventing negative thoughts, blocking out external distractions, and developing a plan of action before the performance begins (Moran, 1996). Examples of psychological routines in tennis, athletics, basketball and soccer have been described in the professional literature (e.g., Samulski & Lopes, 2008; Singer & Anshel, 2006).

In this chapter, we focused on optimal mental state and psychological skills for peak performance in various sports. Continuing with this rationale, mental training techniques/strategies for developing psychological skills were presented. What is the importance of the above parameters?

PSYCHOLOGICAL STRATEGIES BEFORE PERFORMANCE

To achieve an optimal state for best performance, the athlete learns psychological strategies to be applied in his/her pre-competitive and pre-performance activity (routine). Therefore, we will discuss athlete routines (pre-competition and pre performance) used at different stages of competition in order to "bring everything together" towards a "great moment" (Fig.2.2.). In Figure 2.2, the pathway to achieving peak performance is elaborated as compared to the concept presented in Figure 2.1. The main stages towards achieving these great moments (performance) are pre-competitive activity, a pre-performance routine, flow/zone, and post-performance activity.

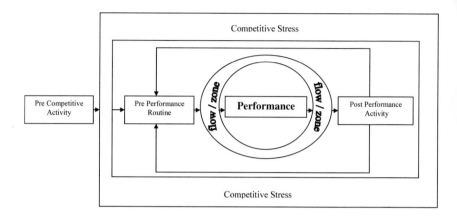

Figure 2.2. Schematic description for "bringing everything together" to peak performance.

Pre-competitive activity-routine (PCA-R) is a special, multifaceted procedure of activity, actions, and thoughts that the athlete carries out before competition (approximately within 24 hours). PCA-R helps athletes achieve a feeling of mental readiness, regulate emotions, and increase self-confidence. The fundamental ground upon which the PCA-R is created is based on the athlete's retrospective positive performance experience. From that experience, the athlete selects different elements of pre-competitive activity, actions, thoughts, and psychological strategies that he/she correlates with successful results in the past. Examples of these are relaxation, self-talk, imagery, habitual clothes, his/her special "place" on the bus, food, interaction with people (e.g., coach, massagist, and psychologist), favorite music, length and content of warm up, and various routines. For example, Michael Phelps' mother Debbie said after he won his eight gold medals at the Beijing Olympic Games: "*Michael had a plan of action. He had a game plan. He knew exactly what he wanted to do.*" (R. Roberts, personal communication on "Good Morning America" on ABC television, August 20th, 2008). In team sports, the athlete relates his/her personal routine with the structure of the team preparation, for example, team meetings, small group meetings (e.g., defense, offense), and team warm up.

The Pre-performance routine (PPR) is an important part of athletic performance, especially in individual sports, with start-attempt (e.g., sprint, jumps and throws in track and field) and in combat sport, with fights/matches (e.g., judo, fencing). The time length of PPR is relatively short, during which the athlete utilizes his/her plan of behavior, thoughts, words, and feelings to prepare for the performance. This helps to build self-confidence, focus attention, and enable a high level of performance. In general, PPR is a scenario of what athlete do, think, and feel in the "zone" prior to a performance.

Lidor (2007) described PPRs in a team sport: "Prior to each free-throw shot, NBA star Karl Malone used the following routine: holding the ball, self-talking, dribbling and focusing attention. David Beckham, the international British soccer star, used a similar routine before each kick, regardless of its distance to the goal" (p. 445). Sometimes, for better preparing for a performance and improving concentration under competitive stress and sounds, athletes "say aloud" the main points of his/her main routines. For example, in the triple jump, "Run up is wide. Keep speed until the end. Do not hurry in a jump." (Saneev, 1975, p.35); in combat sports, the PPR can be "I'm ready, Let's go, concentrate and get aggressive from the beginning." It is of great importance to note that the athlete's routine is highly individualized; do not worry about others; focus on yourself and what is best for you. For example, three-time trap shooting Olympic champion Kim Rhode explains his pre-performance routine: "When I'm standing on the line, I'm singing a song in my head. I'm not thinking, oh my gosh, this is my last bird; oh my gosh, they are ahead of me. I can't miss or I'll be behind. Instead, I'm singing some song, and it helps me with the pressure." (Manhattan shooting excursions: https://www.eliteshooters.com/articles/kimrhode.html)

The athlete demonstrates his/her pre-performance routine automatically and quickly. All psychological strategies that are applied in this time period must be short, punctual, and exactly in the right place and at the right time, with full concentration and high confidence.

Post-performance activity (PPA). After the performance is complete, there is a post-performance analysis and activity in order to prepare the athlete for the next attempt, which might start a few minutes or a few hours after the previous attempt (e.g., jumps in athletics, fights in combat sports). In this time period, the athlete analyzes and self-estimates what has just happened. The athlete must renew his/her optimism (if it was a wrong attempt or fight), by self-talk such as" I have chances, attempt… now relax, and prepare to next…give it 100 percent,…I feel good, I'm ready …Let's do it .. I can do it now." In PPA, a short warm-up can be incorporated, as well as relaxation, self-talk (positive, motivating, instructive), imagery (with positive thinking and visualization ideal technique performance), attention focus, goal setting, and competition simulation (with videotape, rehearse competition situation).

In Chapter 3, we will describe how to learn, practice, and master the above-mentioned skills for achieving for optimal performance. Moreover, we will elaborate on integrating and implementing several psychological skills in typical training programs during the athlete's training process.

REFERENCES

Anshel, M., & Payne, M. (2006). Application of sport psychology for optimal performance in martial arts. In J. Dosil (Ed.), *The sport psychologist's handbook: A guide for sport-specific performance enhancement* (pp. 353-374). Chichester, UK: Wiley.

Bailey, D. (2000, August 10). State of mind paramount in sprinting. *The Globe & Mail*, p. S4.

Blumenstein, B., & Bar-Eli, M. (2001). A five-step approach for biofeedback in sport. *Sportwissenschaft, 4*, 412-424.

Blumenstein, B., Bar-Eli, M., & Collins, D. (2002). Biofeedback training in sport. In B. Blumenstein, M. Bar-Eli, & G. Tenenbaum (Eds.), *Brain and body in sport and exercise: Biofeedback applications in performance enhancement* (pp. 55-76). Chichester, UK: Wiley.

Blumenstein, B., Bar-Eli, M., & Tenenbaum, G. (1995). The augmenting role of biofeedback: Effects of autogenic training, imagery and music on physiological indices and athletic performance. *Journal of Sport Sciences, 13*, 343-354.

Blumenstein, B., Bar-Eli, M., & Tenenbaum, G. (1997). A five-step approach to mental training incorporating biofeedback. *The Sport Psychologist, 11*, 440-453.

Blumenstein, B., & Lidor, R. (2004). Psychological preparation in elite canoeing and kayaking sport programs: Periodization and planning. *Applied Research in Coaching and Athletics Annual, 19*, 24-34.

Blumenstein, B., Lidor, R., & Tenenbaum, G. (2005). Periodization and planning of psychological preparation in elite combat sport programs: The case of judo. *International Journal of Sport and Exercise Psychology, 3*, 7-25.

Blumenstein, B. & Orbach, I. (2012). Biofeedback training at sea. In A. Edmonds & G. Tenenbaum (Eds.), *Case studies in applied psychophysiology: Neurofeedback and biofeedback treatments for advances in human performance* (pp.134-143). Chichester, West Sussex: Wiley-Blackwell.

Blumenstein, B., & Orbach, I. (2012). *Mental practice in sport: Twenty case studies.* New York, NY: Nova Science Publishers.

Blumenstein, B., & Weinstein, Y. (2010). *Psychological skills training: Application to elite sport performance.* Grand Rapids, MI: Ultimate Athlete Concepts.

Blumenstein, B., & Weinstein, Y. (2011). Biofeedback training: Enhancing athletic performance. *Biofeedback, 39*(3), 101-104.

Bois, J., Sarrazin, P., Southon, J., & Boiche, J. (2009). Psychological characteristics and their relation to performance in professional golfers. *The Sport Psychologist*, 23, 252-270.

Bompa, T. (1999). *Theory and methodology of training* (3rd ed.). Dubuque, IA: Kendall/Hunt.

Burke, K. (2006). Using sport psychology to improve basketball performance. In J. Dosil (Ed.), *The sport psychologist's handbook: A guide for sport-specific performance enhancement* (pp. 121-138). Chichester, UK: Wiley.

Burke, K., & Brown, D. (2003). *Sport psychology library series: Basketball.* Morgantown, WV: Fitness Information Technology.

Chung, K., & Lee, K. (1994). *Taekwondo Kyorugi: Olympic style sparring.* Hartford, CT: Turtle Press.

Cogan, K. (2006). Sport psychology in gymnastics. In J. Dosil (Ed.) *The sport psychologist's handbook: A guide for sport-specific performance enhancement* (pp. 641-661). Chichester, UK: Wiley.

Cohn, P. (1990). Pre-performance routines in sport. Theoretical support and practice. *The Sport Psychology*, 4, 301-312.

Cohn, P. (1991). An exploratory study on peak performance in golf. *The Sport Psychologist*, 5, 1-14.

Cotterill, S. (2010). Pre-performance routines in sport: current understanding and future directions. *International Review of Sport and Exercise Psychology*, 3(2), 132-153.

Csikszentmihalyi, M. (1990). *Flow: The psychology of optimal experience.* New York, NY: Harper & Row.

Dosil, J. (2006a). Psychological interventions with football (soccer) teams. In J. Dosil (Ed.), *The sport psychologist's handbook: A guide for sport-specific performance enhancement* (pp. 139-158). Chichester, UK: Wiley.

Dosil, J. (2006b). The psychology of athletics. In J. Dosil (Ed.), *The sport psychologist's handbook: A guide for sport-specific performance enhancement* (pp. 265-284). Chichester, UK: Wiley.

Frey, M., Laguna, P., & Ravizza, K. (2003). Collegiate athlete's mental skill use and perceptions of success: An exploration of the practice and competition settings. *Journal of Applied Sport Psychology*, 15, 115-128.

Garfield, C., & Benett, H. (1984). *Peak performance: Mental training techniques of the world's greatest athletes.* Los Angeles: Tarcher.

Gould, D. (2001). Goal setting for peak performance. In J. Williams (Ed.), *Applied sport psychology: Personal growth to peak performance* (4th ed., pp. 190-205). Mountain View, CA: Mayfield.

Gould, D. (2002). The psychology of Olympic excellence and its development. *Psychology*, *9*, 531-546.

Gould, D., & Damarjian, N. (1998). Mental skills training in sport. In B. Elliot (Ed.), *Applied sport science: Training in sport. International handbook of sport science* (Vol. 3, pp. 69-116). Sussex, England: Wiley.

Gould, D., Deiffenbach, K., & Moffett, A. (2002). Psychological characteristics and their development in Olympic champions. *Journal of Applied Sport Psychology*, 14, 177-209.

Gould, D., Deiffenbach, K., & Moffett, A. (2010, January 5). Psychological characteristics of U.S. Olympic champions. *Cael Sanderson*. Retrieved September 10, 2011, from *http://www.caelsanderson.com/latest-news/psychological-characteristics-of-u-s-olympic-champions*

Gould, D., Eklund, R., & Jackson, S.(1993). Coping strategies used by U.S. Olympic wrestlers. *Research Quarterly for Exercise and Sport*, 64, 83-93.

Gould, D., Flett, R., & Bean, E. (2009). Mental preparation for training and competition. In B. Brewer (Ed.). *Handbook of sport medicine and science: Sport psychology* (pp. 53-63). Chichester, UK: Wiley-Blackwell.

Gould, D., & Maynard, I. (2009). Psychological preparation for the Olympic Games. *Journal of Sport Sciences,* 27(13), 1393-1408.

Gould, D., & Udry, E. (1994). Psychological skills for enhancing performance: Arousal regulating strategies. *Medicine and Science in Sport and Exercise,* 26, 478-485.

Gray, A., & Drewitt, J. (1999). *Flat back four – The tactical game.* London: Boxfree.

Green, E., Green, A., & Walters, E. (1970). Voluntary control of internal states: Psychological and physiological. *Journal of Transpersonal Psychology,* 2, 1-26.

Halliwell, W. (2009). Preparing professional hockey players for play off performance. In R. Schinke (Ed.), *Contemporary sport psychology* (pp. 11-19). New York, NY: Nova Science Publishers.

Hanin, Y. (2000). Individual zones of optimal functioning (IZOF) model: Emotion-performance relationships in sport. In Y. Hanin (Ed.), *Emotions in sport* (pp. 65-89). Champaign, IL: Human Kinetics.

Hanton, S., & Jones, G. (1999). The acquisition and development of cognitive skills and strategies: Making the butterflies fly in formation. *The Sport Psychologist,* 13, 1-21.

Hatzigeorgiadis, A., Theordorakis, Y., & Zourbanos, N. (2004). Self-talk in the swimming pool: The effects of self-talk on thought content and performance in water-polo tasks. *Journal of Applied Sport Psychology,* 16, 138-150.

Henschen, K. (2005). Mental practice – skill oriented. In D. Hackfort, J. Duda, & R. Lidor (Eds.), *Handbook of research in applied sport and exercise psychology: International perspectives* (pp. 19-36). Morgantown, WV: Fitness Information Technology.

Henschen, K., & Cook, D. (2003). Working with professional basketball players. In R. Lidor & K. Henschen (Eds.), *The psychology of team sports* (pp. 143-160). Morgantown, WV: Fitness Information Technology.

Jackson, S. (2000). Joy, fun and flow state in sport. In Y. Hanin (Ed.), *Emotions in sport* (pp. 135-156). Champaign, IL: Human Kinetics.

Jacobson, E. (1930). *Progressive relaxation.* Chicago: University of Chicago Press.

Kerr, B. (2001). Community-based sport psychology. In G. Tenenbaum (Ed.), *The practice of sport psychology* (pp. 155-167). Morgantown, WV: Fitness Information Technology.

Lidor, R. (2007). Preparatory routines in self-paced events. Do they benefit the skilled athletes? Can they help the beginners? In G. Tenenbaum & R. Eklund (Eds.), *Handbook of sport psychology*, (3rd ed., pp. 445-468). Hoboken, NJ: Wiley.

Lidor, R., Blumenstein, B., & Tenenbaum, G. (2007). Periodization and planning of psychological preparation in individual and team sports. In B. Blumenstein, R. Lidor, G. Tenenbaum (Eds.), *Psychology of Sport Training* (pp. 137-161). Oxford, UK: Meyer & Meyer Sports.

Lidor, R., & Singer, R. (2003). Pre-performance routines in self-paced tasks: Developmental and educational considerations. In R. Lidor & K. Henschen (Eds.), *The psychology of team sports* (pp. 69-98). Morgantown, WV: Fitness Information Technology.

Loehr, J. (1984). How to overcome stress and play at your peak all the time. *Tennis*, 66-76.

Mallett, C., & Hanrahan, S. (2004). Elite athletes: Why does the fire burn so brightly? *Psychology of Sport and Exercise, 5*, 183-200.

Manhattan shooting excursions: Interview with three times Olympic Champion – Kim Rhode. *https://www.eliteshooters.com/articles/kimrhode.html*

Moran, A. (1996). *The psychology of concentration in sport performers: A cognitive analysis.* East Sussex, UK: Psychology Press.

Moran, A. (2003). Improving concentration skills in team-sport performance: Focusing techniques for soccer players. In R. Lidor & K. Henschen (Eds.), *The psychology of team sports* (pp. 161-190). Morgantown, WV: Fitness Information Technology.

Morris, T., Spittle, M., & Watt, A. (2005). *Imagery in sport.* Champaign, IL: Human Kinetics.

Michael Phelps, peak performance case study. In the *New York Times,* 8/18/08 (*http://www.squidoo.com/phelps*)

Nideffer, R. (1989). *Attention control training for sport.* Los Gatos, CA: Enhanced Performance Service.

Orlik, T., & Partington, J. (1988). Mental links to excellence. *The Sport Psychologist,* 2, 105-130.

Park, Y., & Seabourne, T. (1997). *Taekwondo techniques and tactics.* Champaign, IL: Human Kinetics.

Pedro, J., & Durbin, W. (2001). *Judo: Techniques and tactics.* Champaign, IL: Human Kinetics.

Philippe, R., & Seiler, R. (2006).Closeness, co-orientation and complementarily in the coach-athlete relationships: What male swimmers say about their male coaches. *Psychology of Sport and Exercise,* 7, 159-171.

Privette, G., & Bundrick, C. (1997). Psychological process of peak, average, and tailing performance in sport. *International Journal of Sport Psychology,* 28, 323-334.

Ravizza, K. (1977). Peak experiences in sport. *Journal of Humanistic Psychology,* 17, 35-40.

Ravizza, K. (2001). Reflections and insights from the field on performance enhancement consultation. In G. Tenenbaum (Ed.), *The practice of sport psychology* (pp. 197-216). Morgantown, WV: Fitness Information Technology.

Rossingh, D. (2011, September 20). Three-time Olympic sailing champion Ainslie seeks a fourth gold in London. Bloomberg. Retrieved December 10, 2011, from *http://mobile.bloomberg.com/news/2011-09-20/three-time-olympic-sailing-champion.*

Rushall, B. S. (1989). Sport psychology: The key to sporting excellence. *International Journal of Sport Psychology,* 20, 165-190.

Samulski, D., & Lopes, M. (2008). Counseling Brazilian athletes during the Olympic Games in Athens 2004: Important issues and intervention techniques. *International Journal of Sport and Exercise Psychology,* 6, 277-286.

Schack, T., Whitmarsh, B., Pike, R., & Redden, C. (2005) Routines. In J. Taylor, & G. Wilson (Eds.), *Applying sport psychology. Four perspectives* (pp.137-150). Champaign, IL: Human Kinetics.

Schultz, J. (1932). *Das autogene Training* (Autogenic training), Stuttgart, Germany: Thieme.

Sheard, M., & Golby, J. (2006).Effect of a psychological skills training program on swimming performance and positive psychological development. *International Journal of sport and exercise psychology*, 4(2), 149-169.

Singer, R. (1988). Strategies and metastrategies in learning and performing self-paced athletic skills. *Sport Psychologist*, 2, 49-68.

Singer, R., & Anshel, M. (2006). An overview of interventions in sport. In J. Dosil (Ed.) *The sport psychologist's handbook: A guide for sport-specific performance enhancement*, (pp.63-88), Chichester, UK: Wiley.

Singer, R., Hausenblas, H., & Janelle, C. (Eds.). (2001). *Handbook of Sport psychology* (2nd ed.). New York: Wiley.

Statler, T., & Henschen, K. (2009). A sport psychology service delivery model for developing and current track and field athletes and coaches. In T. Hung, R. Lidor, & D. Hackfort (Eds.), *Psychology of sport excellence* (pp. 25-31). Morgantown, WV: Fitness Information Technology.

Suinn, R. (1984). Imagery and sports. In W. Straub & J. Williams (Eds.), *Cognitive sport psychology* (pp. 253-272). Lansing, NY: Sport Science Associates.

Suinn, R. (1993). Imagery. In R. Singer, M. Murphey, & L. Tennant (Eds.), *Handbook of research on sport psychology* (p. 492-510). New York, NY: Macmillan.

Thomas, P. (2001). Professional practice in sport psychology: Developing programs with golfers and orienteers. In G. Tenenbaum (Ed.), *The practice of sport psychology* (pp. 255-272). Morgantown, WV: Fitness Information Technology.

Vealey, R. (1988). Future directions in psychological skills training. *Sport Psychology*, 2, 318-336.

Vealey, R. (2007). Mental skills training in sport. In G. Tenenbaum & R. Eklund (Eds.), *Handbook of sport psychology* (3rd ed., pp. 287-309). New York: Wiley.

Vealey, R., & Greenleaf, C. (2001). Seeing is believing: Understanding and using imagery in sport. In J. Williams (Ed.), *Applied sport psychology: Personal growth to peak performance* (4th ed., pp. 247-283). Mountain View, CA: Mayfield.

Vealey, R., & Greenleaf, C. (2006). Seeing is believing: Understanding and using imagery in sport. In J. Williams (Ed.), *Applied sport psychology: Personal growth to peak performance* (5th ed., pp. 306-348). Boston, MA: McGraw-Hill.

Vernacchia, R. (2003). Working with individual team sports: The psychology of track and field. In R. Lidor & K. Henschen (Eds.), *The psychology of team sports* (pp. 235-265). Morgantown, WV: Fitness Information Technology.

Vernacchia, R., & Statler, T. (2005). *The psychology of high performance track and field*. Mountain View, CA: Track and Field News.

Weinberg, R. (1988). *The mental advantage: Developing your psychological skills in tennis*. Champaign, IL: Leisure Press.

Williams, J., & Harris, D. (2001). Relaxation and energizing techniques for regulation of arousal. In J. Williams (Ed.), *Applied sport psychology: Personal growth to peak performance* (4th ed., pp. 229-246). Mountain View, CA: Mayfield.

Williams, J., & Krane, V. (2001). Psychological characteristics of peak performance. In J. Williams (Ed.), *Applied sport psychology: Personal growth to peak performance* (4th ed., pp. 162-178). Mountain View, Mayfield.

Wooden, J. (1980). *Practical modern basketball* (2nd ed.). New York: Wiley.

Young, J. & Pearce, A. (2009).Attributes of champion female tennis players and challenges faced by aspirants. *Medical Science Tennis*, 2009, 14(2).

Zaichkowsky, L. (1975). Combating stress: What about relaxation and biofeedback? *Movement*, 1, 309-312.

Zaichkowsky, L. (2009). A case for a new sport psychology: Applied psychophysiology and FMRI neuroscience. In R. Schinke (Ed.), *Contemporary sport psychology* (pp. 21-32). New York, NY: Nova Science Publishers.

Chapter 3

DEVELOPING PSYCHOLOGICAL SKILLS: THE THREE-DIMENSIONAL APPROACH

SUMMARY

In this chapter, we present an innovative psychological skills program that was developed based on our personal consulting experience. The approach is composed of three dimensions: Learning, Modification, and Application (LMA). The approach is integrated into the athlete's psychological preparation and is based on the periodization principle. Using real examples, we will demonstrate the internal structure of psychological skills training as used by athletes at all skill levels.

THE THREE-DIMENSIONAL APPROACH: LMA

The validity and the rationale of the LMA approach is based on the periodization principle of the theory and methodology of sport training, on the scientific research in the area of PST, and on our extended experience of more than 30 years. The LMA approach is a training process in which its main objective is developing psychological skills and transforming them from the laboratory to the athlete's/team pre-competitive and pre-performance routines. At the end of the LMA training process the acquired skills are characterized by the following: (1) The skills and their application are specific to the sport discipline (e.g., relaxation or concentration for a combat match is different than relaxation or concentration for a sprint or golf); (2) The application time of the skills during competition is significantly shorter (e.g., from a few seconds to a few minutes); (3) In competitive events the skills are used as a combination of skills, in contrast to the learning stage in which each skill is practiced individually; (4) The psychological skills package is stable under stressful conditions, allowing the athlete to achieve mental consistency within his or her routine; (5) The skills package is tailored based on the athlete's personality and sport needs. When applying this approach, the current physical and psychological state of the athlete, as well as the specific preparation phase of the training program, should be taken into account (Balague, 2000; Blumenstein, Lidor, & Tenenbaum, 2005, 2007; Blumenstein & Weinstein, 2010; Blumenstein & Orbach, 2012; Holliday, Burton, Sun, Hammermeister, Naylor & Freigang, 2008). The LMA approach includes the following three stages: Learning, Modification, and Application (Blumenstein & Orbach, 2012). In the **Learning** stage athletes acquire fundamental psychological techniques in a laboratory setting, namely in controlled and sterile conditions, in order to enable the athletes to learn the basic foundations of each strategy. Moreover, towards the end of this stage, athletes train under light (1-2) stress distractions (see Table 3.1). The psychological strategies are practiced under the following situations:

- *Stress Distraction level 1:* The skills are learned under ordinary, sterile situations in laboratory settings.
- *Stress Distraction level 2:* The skills are practiced under both positive and negative motivation. Examples of Positive motivation statements are "good work" and "you are great," while "negative" motivation statements are "what are you doing today?," "you are having a bad day," and "again a mistake?"

Table 3.1. Stress distraction scale used in the LMA approach

Stress Distraction Level	Description
1*	Ordinary laboratory settings
2	Verbal motivation (positive/negative)
3	Performance under precise demands – graded performance levels
4	Reward / punishment for performance
5	Performance under "true" competition noise (competition audio clips)
6	Performance under "true" competition sights (competition video clips)
7	Various combinations of levels 1-6

*The scale ranges from 1, representing light stress, to 7, representing high stress distractions

In the **Modified** stage, athletes continue to develop psychological skills under challenging stress distractions (3-4, see Table 3.1). The objectives of this stage are to perform more short psychological strategies, quickly and precisely, under stress distractions in the laboratory and training settings. The psychological strategies are practiced under the following situations:

- *Stress Distraction level 3:* Mental performance with specific demands, such as a time limit: Getting into a relaxation and concentration mode within a time limit of one, two, three, four, and five minutes. Quality demands, which is the ability to concentrate (or relax) with a concrete number value (delta), in HR, EMG, and GSR/EDA measurements.
- *Stress Distraction level 4:* In this level, skills are continued to be practiced under the demands of level 3, with a new condition: Success is rewarded, and failure is penalized based on an agreement we established with the athlete before practicing stress distraction level 4, which is preserved throughout all stages.

The skills are adapted in line with technical-tactical purposes and the sport's requirements. Moreover, the mental practice is provided initially in the lab and finally in the training setting. In the **Applied** stage, psychological techniques are practiced in the laboratory under stress distraction levels 5-7 (see Table 3.1). The psychological strategies are practiced under the following situations:

- *Stress Distraction level 5*: The athlete practices his or her mental performance accompanied by real-life competition sound clips.
- *Stress Distraction level 6:* Mental training while opponents and self-video competition clips are displayed.
- *Stress Distraction level 7:* Combinations of levels 1-6 dynamically defined by current conditions.

In addition, the mental strategies are part of the pre-competitive and pre-performance routines and are applied in actual practice sessions and competitions where the athletes are exposed to more authentic situations and real-life distractions. The uniqueness of this stage is the ability of the athlete to apply the psychological strategies quickly and effectively in training and competition. Moreover, the strategies are integrated with the technical, tactical, and physical demands of competition and sport. For example, initially, muscle relaxation techniques are taught and practiced for long periods of time (e.g., intervals of five to ten min) within a laboratory setting, in a quiet and distraction-free environment.

Then, relaxation is performed with stress factors (noises, comments, films) for short periods of time (e.g., intervals of one to three min). Eventually, relaxation becomes more sport specific, helping the athletes cope with the specific technical-tactical demands of the training program and competition (e.g., rapid relaxation before matches and games, and between attempts). The same logic and sequence is provided for other psychological techniques, such as imagery and attention-focusing strategies, self-talk, and goal setting.

PERIODIZATION AND THE LMA APPROACH

According to the theory and methodology of sport training, a basic and fundamental principle of athlete preparation is training periodization (e.g., Bompa, 1999; Bompa & Haff, 2009; Carrera & Bompa, 2007; Zatsiorsky, 1995). Periodization is a planning tool for developing the athlete's training program. Basically, the periodization has three major phases: preparation (general and specific), competition, and transition. When applying our psychological program, our main focus is on the incorporation of the mental session with the athlete's training program, while linking it with the other preparations: the physical, technical, and tactical. Moreover, we modify the mental sessions based on the volume and intensity of the athlete's physical training.

The periodization principle adds a planning timeline tool to the athlete's overall preparations and therefore is used as a guideline to PST training-especially in the LMA approach (see Table 3.2).

Table 3.2. The three major phases of training periodization and the LMA approach

LMA Approach			
Learning Stage	*Modification Stage*	*Application Stage*	
General Preparation	Specific Preparation		
Preparation Phase		*Competitive Phase*	*Transition Phase*
Training Periodization Phases			

THE LEARNING STAGE OF THE LMA APPROACH

The Learning stage begins with the **general preparation** of the Preparation phase (see Table 3.2). During the Learning stage, athletes practice the basic psychological strategies, such as muscle relaxation, concentration, imagery, biofeedback training, and self-talking. This process is usually accompanied by the biofeedback control using physiological measures (HR = Heart Rate; EMG – electromyography, EDA/GSR – Electro Dermal Activity/Galvanic Skin Response). At the end of this stage the athlete is exposed to "light" stress distractions (levels 1-2 in Table 3.1), such as verbal positive and negative comments, and self-talk. The objectives of this stage are to learn and perform basic psychological strategies exactly under "light" stress distractions in a laboratory setting. The length of the stage can last up to two months (i.e., seven to eight sessions).

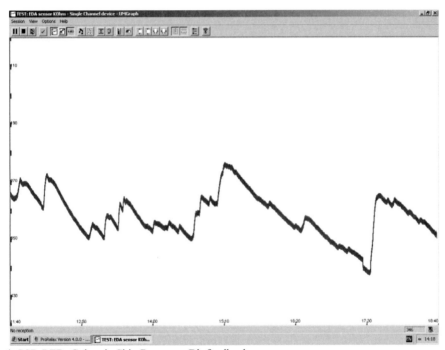

* GSR BFB: Galvanic Skin Response Biofeedback

Figure 3.1. The beginning of the Learning stage: GSR BFB* data of an athlete under stress distraction level "1" while practicing relaxation skills.

In the following example, we present two biofeedback data of an athlete practicing muscle relaxation, representing the initial and the final part of the learning stage. As can be seen in Figure 3.1, the athlete is able to achieve relaxation only for a short period of time (e.g., 20 sec – 2 min) and in an inconsistent manner. The data indicate relatively "weak" relaxation skills in a sterile situation. More specifically, when the line goes down, it indicates the ability of the athlete to relax. On the other hand, when the line goes up, it indicates the inability of the athlete to self-regulate his or her mental state. The lower the line, the better self-regulation, especially relaxation skills.

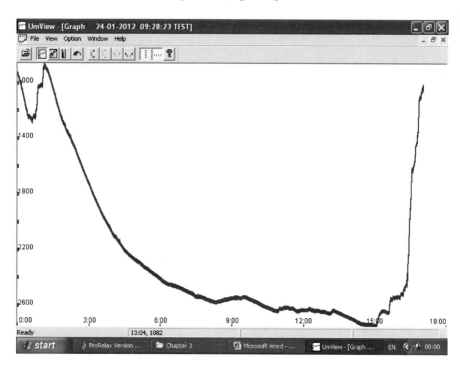

Figure 3.2. One of the final sessions of the Learning Stage: GSR BFB data under stress distraction level 2 while practicing relaxation skills for 15 minutes.

In Figure 3.2, the athletes perform muscle relaxation relatively effectively and achieve the session's goal, which is muscle relaxation under "light" stress distractions (e.g., negative statements such as "you are having a bad day," "you are weak-willed today," and "the referee is against you"). As can be seen by the graph, the delta of 15 minutes' relaxation is 1700kΩ (the delta is the difference between GSR baseline of 900kΩ and the lowest GSR of 2600kΩ that the athlete achieves during the relaxation). These data demonstrate excellent relaxation skills in a laboratory setting under stress distraction level 2. The same principle is used with other strategies (see Table 3.3).

In addition, in the learning stage, we use different multimedia games in which variables of difficulty (1=difficult, 10=easy) and environment change (progress of the story) are applied (see Figure 3.3). These dynamic games are based on an animated principle in which the athlete uses relaxation and concentration skills to move the main subject (fish, man, athlete) forward from the left to the right side. During this process, the main subject is transformed to other forms that can be seen on the PC screen.

A fragment of this game, "Evolution," is presented below. The man in the picture is being transformed into an astronaut through the relaxation/concentration skills.

Figure 3.3. The Learning stage: An example of the "Evolution" multimedia game.

At the end of this stage, the athlete masters relaxation, concentration, and imagery skills.

The use of the multimedia games serve several purposes: The athlete and consultant receive objective data on the learning progress; the data serve as an additional tool for the psychological skills training; the athletes enjoy the process due to the variety of the games and the possibility of different stress distraction levels. An example is an athlete who completed the "Fish" game, stress distraction level 5 (relatively difficult), in 45 seconds at the end of the learning stage.

THE MODIFICATION STAGE OF THE LMA APPROACH

This stage is applied parallel to the **specific preparation** (see Table 3.2). The main objective of the **specific preparation** of the preparation phase is to further develop the athlete's physical ability according to the unique physical and physiological characteristics of a specific sport (Blumenstein et al., 2007; Bompa, 1999; Bompa & Haff, 2009; Carrera & Bompa, 2007).

Therefore, during the mental session of the Modification stage, the focus is on concentration and imagery techniques, in which the athlete visualizes technical elements of him- or herself and his or her opponents under moderate stress distractions (levels 3-4 in Table 3.1).

This means practicing PST under precise demands, such as graded perfection levels (e.g., time limits, delta goals of GSR/ EMG/ HR values) and reward/punishment for good/bad performance. An example of a graded perfection level is asking the athlete to perform within a time limit (e.g., deep relaxation within a time limit of 30 sec, 1 min, 2 min; fast concentration during 10, 20, 30 sec).

Another stress factor can be achieving delta goals of GSR/EMG/HR values such as attaining EMG from the frontalis (forehead) muscle from 2.6μV to 1.2μV within a time limit of 10 and 20 sec.

In addition, an example of reward/punishment can be when the athlete is punished if he or she does not achieve a specific value/goal in deep relaxation within a time limit of 30 sec, 1 min, 2 min, or fast concentration during 10, 20, 30 sec. In Figure 3.4, the athlete performs some relaxation exercises within certain time limits.

In Figure 3.4, the athlete can achieve relaxation in a relatively shorter period of time (three min) compared to the previous stage.

The delta is approximately 100kΩ, which indicates the ability of the athlete to self-regulate under demands such as time limit and reward/punishment (stress distraction levels 3-4). To perform this exercise successfully, the athlete should master the self-regulation skills at a high level.

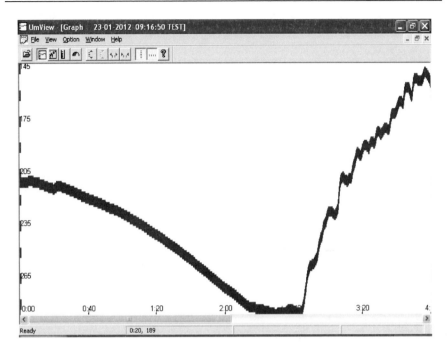

Figure 3.4. Modification stage: An example of relaxation during three minutes followed by a one-minute imagery.

Finally, during basketball practice, the athlete uses short relaxation/concentration/imagery while he or she is in the substitution area, waiting for his or her turn to play.

At the end of the Modification stage, mental support during training is accompanied by different portable BFB devices, such as the Mind Master[801] and Stress Master[802] by Atlas Ltd. (skin response monitors, reflecting variations in sweat gland activity). These devices can be used for homework, practice, and competitions.

In addition, in this stage, the "double-feedback" procedure can be used (Blumenstein, Bar-Eli, & Collins, 2002; Blumenstein & Weinstein, 2011). The objective of this procedure is to teach the athlete regulation skills for controlling facial expressions during pre-performance and pre-competitive routines. This approach indicates the possibility of using BFB together with behavioral reactions, in order to affect the athlete's opponent.

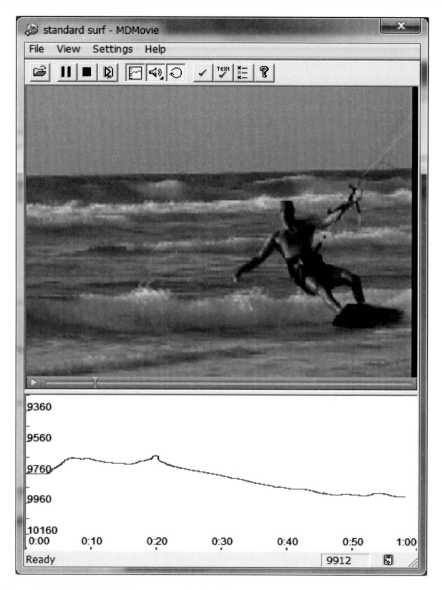

Figure 3.5. The Modification stage: Windsurfing multimedia game under time limit.

In Figures 3.5 and 3.6, the athlete practices his or her self-regulation skills while viewing a sport-specific scene. The demand of this game is performing three jumps (as can be seen in Figure 3.5) within one minute.

Figure 3.6. The Modification stage: Windsurfing multimedia game in progress (jumping surf).

THE APPLICATION STAGE OF THE LMA APPROACH

This stage is provided mainly in the competition phase (see Table 3.1). In the **Competition** phase, the intensity of the performed technical elements increases and the repetitions decrease while the total time of training decreases. A variety of real environmental factors related to the specific sport are considered. In addition, the tactical preparation of the athlete is a significant factor in this phase. Taking the above into account, during mental training sessions in the Application stage, the athlete practices concentration and imagery techniques with competitive stress (e.g., use of recorded competitive films and noises, stress distraction levels 5-7), as well as arousal regulation with different stress distractions. For example, one of the exercises that the athlete practices in the laboratory at this stage is "relaxation-excitation" waves. The athlete begins this exercise by watching video scenes from competitive situations in which he or she competed. The scenes are presented on the VCR (Video Camera Recorder) screen, followed by one min of relaxation and two to five min of imagery scenes of competitive segment. The cycle is finalized with one min of relaxation. The entire process is accompanied by the continuous measurements of GSR BFB. To strengthen the link between the mental sessions and performance during competition, beyond imagery clarity, we require that the athlete match the imagery time to the actual competition time (a judoka images for five min-a match lasts five min in competition; imagery for individual rhythmic gymnasts lasts for about 1:30 min; in Taekwondo the athlete images three periods of two min each, with a one-min pause between periods).

Figure 3.7 demonstrates a swimmer who mentally prepares for the start of a 50-meter event. The swimmer begins with relaxation for 30 seconds and then imagines the start of the event as a reaction to the command "step up, take your mark, go." The cycle is repeated three times. In Figure 3.7, we can see that the athlete was successful in the first and third attempts but not in the second attempt. During the second attempt, the athlete was not able to focus and imagine his start. In other words, the second excitation values of the athlete were lower (approximately 405kΩ) compared to the first and third excitation values (approximately 375kΩ).

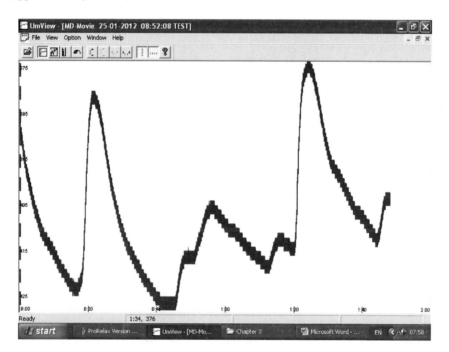

Figure 3.7. The Application stage: Relaxation-excitation waves of a swimmer practicing the start of a 50-meter event.

Table 3.3. Development of psychological strategies based on the LMA approach and the Periodization principle

Psychological Techniques / LMA Stages	TRAINING PHASES			
	Preparation		**Competition**	**Transition**
	General	**Specific**		
	Learning Stage	Modification Stage	Application Stage	
Setting	Lab	Lab-Training	Lab-Training-Competition	Lab
Using stress distracters	1, 2	3, 4	5, 6, 7	
Relaxation	Muscle relaxation (basic version)	Relaxation in practice (short version)	Relaxation in pre-competitive and pre-performance routine (rapid)	Relaxation for recovery
Imagery	From external imagery to internal imagery	Internal imagery of technical-tactical aspects of performance	Imagery is part of pre-competitive and pre-performance routine. Imagery of key technical elements of performance.	
Self-talk	Self-talk before and during training	Stop negative thoughts in practice and competition	Key words, stop negative thoughts in competition	
Concentration	Variety of concentration exercises	Fast and intensive concentration in practice	Concentration in pre-competitive and pre-performance routine. Concentration during performance.	
Goal-setting	Training goal and plan	Technical, tactical and positive attitude goals	Performance goals	Long-term goals

At the end of the Modification stage, the athlete is able to bring the learned self-regulation skills together and use them in his or her pre-performance routine in training and competition. During the process of transferring the skills to a real-life competitive event, the athlete initially uses the skills in several lower-level competitions to assess the effectiveness of his or her pre-performance routine. Based on this, the athlete corrects and adjusts his or her skills when necessary in order to prepare for more significant main competitions.

In the transition phase, mental recovery, such as relaxation, listening to music, and breathing exercises, are used, incorporating BFB devices.

Table 3.3 demonstrates the important elements of the LMA approach. First, the LMA stages connect with the periodization principle in the athlete's training program. Second, throughout the process, the athlete is exposed to stress distracters that prepare him or her for a better and easier transition from practice to competition. Third, the mental training is conducted initially in the lab and at the final stage in training and competition. Finally, characteristics typical of all psychological strategies that are being learned based on the LMA approach are:

- The length of the mental strategies becomes shorter as the athlete progresses through the LMA stages;
- The mental strategies become more sport specific from stage to stage;
- At the end of the LMA approach, the strategies are established as an integral part of the pre-competitive and pre-performance routines;
- The routines are individualized for the athlete's needs and competitive conditions.

The LMA approach is accompanied by BFB and physiological measurements. Therefore, the athlete is able to progress relatively quicker and more effectively throughout the training process. The athlete observes his or her results in each stage and therefore is able to better understand his or her concrete goals in the way to achieving excellence.

This book mainly focuses on "what" and "how" sport psychology consultants advise athletes in order for them to achieve the best results. The field of sport psychology is based on a serious and valid scientific/theoretical background. This theoretical knowledge must be developed in order to be applied in the athlete's daily practice and competition. We suggest the LMA approach as a way to achieve this goal.

In Figure 3.8, we present the relationship between psychological skills training (PST) and athletic performance, which includes the development of psychological skills and applying them in pre-competitive activity and pre-performance routines. The LMA approach is a guideline for developing psychological skills and integrates them into the athlete's preparations.

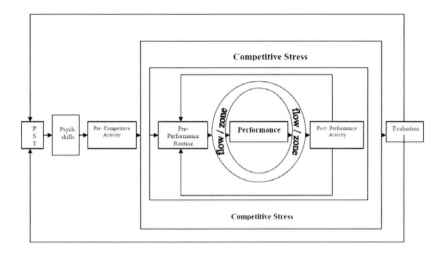

Figure 3.8. Schematic description of the relationship between Psychological Skills Training (PST) and athletic performance.

CONCLUSION

In *Psychological Skills in Sport: Training and Application*, we share our individualized approach to providing sport psychology support in order to produce successful athletes. To achieve this goal, attention should be paid to the following points:

- PST should be an integral part of athlete's training practice. Future research should investigate the effectiveness of this integration.
- The development of PST should be based on the Periodization principle.
- Basic psychological strategies should be learned in two versions: Long version for pre-competitive activity and short version for pre-performance routine.
- To measure the athlete's progress objectively, sport psychology consultants should use psychophysiology measures/norms. This way, the sport psychology consultant will be provided with methodology to quantify baseline abilities in psychological skills, monitor changes, and

enable the training of athletes to self-regulate their bodies, thoughts, feelings and actions (Zaichkovsky, 2009).

- The sport psychology consultant must have more information and knowledge on the theory and methodology of sport training. Moreover, the consultant must have excellent communication and education skills for explaining to the coach and athlete the importance of PST in daily practice. In addition, psychological support should be integrated into training and competition.
- The coach must understand the necessity of mentally preparing his or her athlete for competition. This is done by using the services of sport psychology consultant as part of the professional staff.
- Both the consultant and coach must be mentally tough, especially during competitive stress, and therefore they must develop their own psychological skills.

In this book, we attempt to provide our own experience and philosophy, which can assist in answering the relevant issues within sport psychology.

REFERENCES

Balague, G. (2000). Periodization of psychological skills training. *Journal of Science and Medicine in Sport, 3*(3), 230-237.

Blumenstein, B., Bar-Eli, M., & Collins, D. (2002). Biofeedback training in sport. In B. Blumenstein, M. Bar-Eli, & G. Tenenbaum (Eds.), *Brain and body in sport and exercise: Biofeedback applications in performance enhancement* (pp. 55-76). Chichester, UK: Wiley.

Blumenstein, B., Lidor, R., & Tenenbaum, G. (2005). Periodization and planning of psychological preparation in elite combat sport programs: The case of judo. *International Journal of Sport and Exercise Psychology, 3*, 7-25.

Blumenstein, B., Lidor, R., & Tenenbaum, G. (2007) (Eds.). *Psychology of sport training*. Oxford, UK: Meyer & Meyer Sport.

Blumenstein, B., & Orbach, I. (2012). *Mental practice in sport: Twenty case studies*. New York, NY: Nova Science Publishers.

Blumenstein, B., & Weinstein, Y. (2010). *Psychological skills training: Application to elite sport performance*. Grand Rapids, MI: Ultimate Athlete Concepts.

Blumenstein, B., & Weinstein, Y. (2011). Biofeedback training: Enhancing athletic performance. *Biofeedback,* 39(3), 101-104

Bompa, T. (1999). *Periodization: Theory and methodology of training* (4th ed.). Champaign, IL: Human Kinetics.

Bompa, T., & Haff, G. (2009). *Periodization: Theory and methodology of training* (5th ed.). Champaign, IL: Human Kinetics.

Carrera, M., & Bompa, T. (2007). Theory and methodology of training: General perspectives. In B. Blumenstein, R. Lidor, & G. Tenenbaum (Eds.). *Psychology of sport training* (pp. 19-39). Oxford, UK: Meyer & Meyer Sport.

Holliday, B., Burton, D., Sun, G., Hammermeister, J., Naylor, S., & Freigang, D. (2008). Building the better mental training mousetrap: Is periodization a more systematic approach to promoting performance excellence? *Journal of Applied Sport Psychology,* 20, 199-219.

Zaichkowsky, L. (2009). A case for a new sport psychology: Applied psychophysiology and Fmri neuroscience. In R. Schinke (Ed.), *Contemporary sport psychology* (pp. 21-32). New York, NY: Nova Science Publishers.

Zatsiorsky, V. (1995). *Science and practice of strength training.* Champaign, IL: Human Kinetics.

ABOUT THE AUTHORS

Dr. Boris Blumenstein is the Director of the Department of Behavioral Sciences at the Ribstein Center for Sport Medicine Sciences and Research, Wingate Institute, Israel. He received his Ph.D. in Sport Psychology in 1980, from the All Union Institute for Research in Sport, Department of Sport Psychology, Moscow, Russia (former USSR). His extensive experience in sport psychology spans some 30 years, culminating in applied work at the elite level. He was a sport psychology consultant for the Soviet national and Olympic teams, and since 1990, for the Israeli national and Olympic teams (including the delegations to the Atlanta 1996, Sydney 2000, Athens 2004, and Beijing 2008 Olympics). He is author and coauthor of over 90 refereed journal articles and book chapters, mainly in the area of sport and exercise psychology. Dr. Blumenstein is the senior editor of the book *Brain and Body in Sport and Exercise: Biofeedback Applications in Performance Enhancement*, published by Wiley (2002), and *Psychology of Sport Training*, published by Meyer & Meyer Sport (2007). He is the chief author of *Psychological Skills Training: Application to Elite Sport Performance*, published by Ultimate Athlete Concepts (2010), and *Mental Practice in Sport: Twenty Case Studies*, published by Nova Science Publishers (2012). He has also given more than 80 scientific presentations at international and national conferences and workshops. His current research interests include mental skills training for enhanced performance, stress-performance relationships, the effectiveness of different mental interventions, and athletic competition readiness. In addition, he is a member of the Managing Council of the Israeli Biofeedback Society and the past president of the Israeli Society for Sport Psychology.

Dr. Iris Orbach is a researcher and a sport psychology consultant in the Department of Behavioral Sciences at the Ribstein Center for Sport Medicine

Sciences and Research, Wingate Institute, Israel. She received her Ph.D. in Sport Psychology in 1999, from the University of Florida, Department of Sport and Exercise Sciences, in Gainesville, Florida, USA. She worked as an assistant professor for eight years in the Department of Sport, Fitness and Leisure Studies at Salem State University, Salem, Massachusetts, USA. In addition to teaching, Dr. Orbach has published numerous articles and book chapters and has given presentations at national and international conferences on topics related to sport psychology. She is the coauthor of the book *Mental Practice in Sport: Twenty Case Studies*, published by Nova Science Publishers, 2012. Her current research interests include stress-performance relationships, children and motivation in sport, and the effectiveness of various mental training practices. Dr. Orbach uses her psychology skills as a consultant for athletes at all skill levels. In her free time, Dr. Orbach enjoys running, bicycling, swimming, weight lifting, and all kind of fitness activities.

INDEX

videotape, 29
visualization, 20, 29

W

walking, 19, 20

water, ix, 32
Western countries, 7
worry, 29
wrestling, 18, 22, 23